HAL LEONARD
GUITAR METHOD

MUSIC THEORY
BY TOM KOLB

D0899799

To access audio visit:
www.halleonard.com/mylibrary

Enter Code
3767-3474-9919-1972

ISBN 978-0-634-06651-1

Visit Hal Leonard Online at
www.halleonard.com

Contact us:
Hal Leonard
7777 West Bluemound Road
Milwaukee, WI 53213
Email: info@halleonard.com

In Europe, contact:
Hal Leonard Europe Limited
42 Wigmore Street
Marylebone, London, W1U 2RN
Email: info@halleonardeurope.com

In Australia, contact:
Hal Leonard Australia Pty. Ltd.
4 Lentara Court
Cheltenham, Victoria, 3192 Australia
Email: info@halleonard.com.au

CONTENTS

INTRODUCTION

You are holding in your hands a unique book—a complete music theory method designed specifically for guitarists. While there are many music theory books on the market, most focus on the piano keyboard and the grand staff. In *Music Theory for the Guitarist*, every concept, exercise, and musical example is guitar-specific.

In regard to the pace of the materials presented, the first few chapters of the book deal with fundamental terms, but from that point on, there is no specific sequence as far as level of difficulty. There are valuable concepts to be learned in every chapter, regardless of your playing level. So feel free to jump in anywhere, or simply use it as a handy reference guide. At any time if you come across an unfamiliar musical term, simply look it up in the index on page 94 to find the place in the book where it is explained.

Quizzes and eartraining drills appear periodically throughout the book. These are designed to help "cement" the material brought forth in each chapter. The answers are located in the answer keys at the back of the book.

I truly hope you find this book helpful. Good luck, and have fun with your music.

—Tom Kolb

ABOUT THE RECORDING

Many of the examples in this book are demonstrated on the accompanying audio. These are identified with an audio icon. Some feature a backup rhythm section (wherever appropriate). For these tracks, the featured guitar is mixed hard right. This allows you to isolate the part, play along with the entire mix, or, by adjusting the balance to the left, play along with just the rhythm section. Listen to the audio track to tune your guitar to the recording.

Recording Credits:

All guitars, bass, keyboards, and drum programming: Tom Kolb

All musical examples composed and arranged by Tom Kolb

Assistant Recording Engineer: Dan Brownfield

ABOUT THE AUTHOR

A veteran of over 6,000 live performances and recording sessions world wide, Tom Kolb has found himself in just about every musical situation imaginable. He currently maintains a busy schedule of gigs and sessions with a wide variety of artists (including his own band, The Gurus) in the Los Angeles area and abroad.

An instructor at the world famous Musicians Institute (G.I.T.) since 1989, Tom is also the author of the instructional books *Amazing Phrasing, Modes for Guitar,* and *Chord Progressions (101 Patterns from Folk to Funk)*, all available through Hal Leonard. He has also written countless magazine articles and currently holds a position as an Associate Editor and monthly columnist for *Guitar One* magazine. In addition to his playing and writing career, Tom is also the featured artist on many Star Licks and Hal Leonard instructional videos and DVDs, including: *50 Licks Rock Style, Fender Stratocaster Greats, Modes for the Lead Guitarist, the Starter Series, Best of Lennon and McCartney for Electric Guitar, Famous Rock Guitar Riffs and Solos, '60s Psychedelic Guitar, Advanced Chords and Rhythms*, and the *Hal Leonard Guitar Method*.

ACKNOWLEDGMENTS

I'd like to thank my wife Hedy and my daughter Flynnie for their unconditional love and support; my parents for their encouragement in my formative years; Hal Leonard Corporation; all at *Guitar One* magazine; the staff and students at Musicians Institute, Hollywood; and all the musicians I have had the privilege of playing with over the years.

CHAPTER 1: THE FRETBOARD

FRETBOARD LAYOUT

As this is a guitar-specific book, let's start with an overview of the guitar fretboard:

Fig. 1

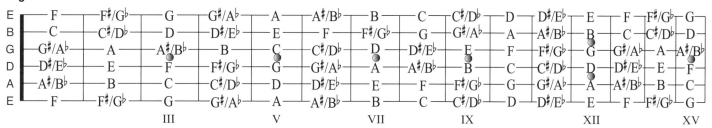

The guitar is a fretted, six-string instrument, tuned low to high: E–A–D–G–B–E. The frets represent *half-step* increments (see Chapter 4, Intervals), so playing along one string (from "open" to the twelfth fret) produces all twelve pitches of the *chromatic scale* (see Chapter 12). The twelfth fret represents an octave (see Chapter 4, Intervals) above the starting point (open string), at which the pitches start over again, until ending at frets 21 or 22 (on most electric guitars). Unlike on a piano, the same note can be played at several different points on the guitar. This is demonstrated below.

Fig. 2

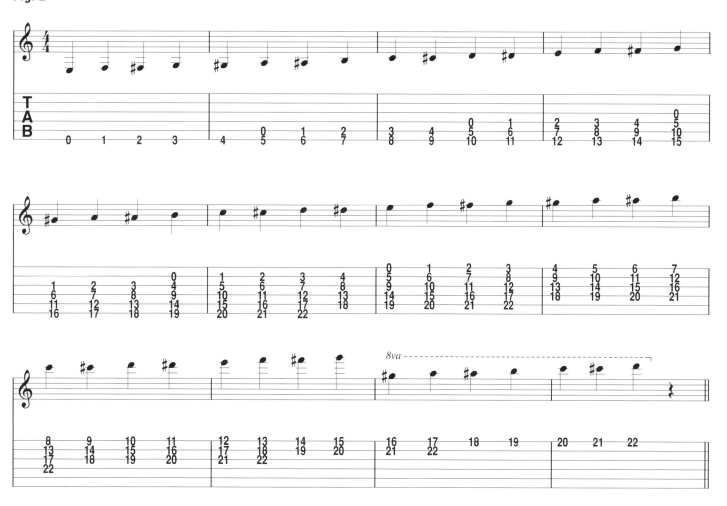

Learning the names of the open strings is easy, but memorizing all of the notes on the fretboard can be a long and difficult process. Here's a great warm-up exercise to assist you in achieving that goal: Choose any note and play it once on each string (where it's located between the open string and the eleventh fret), from the low E to the high E and back down again. Start slowly at first, gradually increasing the tempo. Do this for a minute or so, then repeat the process an octave up (between frets 12 and 22). Do this every day (with a different note), and in no time you'll be able to locate any pitch on the guitar immediately—truly an invaluable skill. This exercise is demonstrated below with the note A.

Fig. 3A

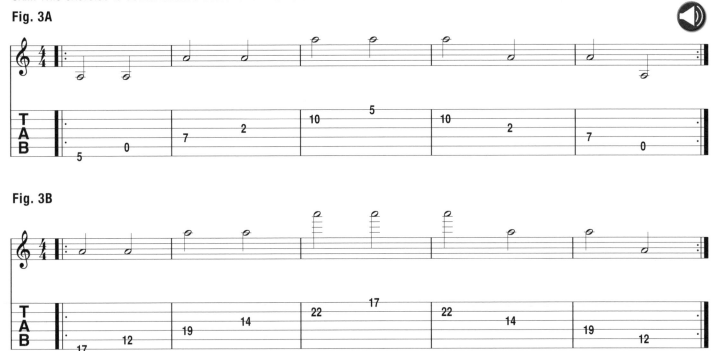

Fig. 3B

Here's an important revelation that many overlook: The tuning system used for guitar follows a pattern of ascending, perfect-fourth *intervals* (see Chapter 4, Intervals): low E up to A (4th); A to D (4th); D to G (4th); G to B (major 3rd, the exception); and B to E (4th). It goes to follow that parallel notes (at the same fret) on adjacent strings (other than the G and B strings), are also perfect fourths (major thirds on the G and B strings) anywhere on the neck. This information provides a vital clue for deciphering intervals (and other note relationships) on the fretboard. (This process is discussed in detail in Chapter 4.)

TUNING

Whether you choose to tune your guitar to another instrument (such as piano), or an electronic tuner, you should always fine-tune your guitar to *itself* once you've finished. Here's a step-by-step process to help you double-check your guitar's tuning:

Use the A string as the master pitch source. Play the open A string and fret the low E string at fret 5. Then adjust the tuning of the low E string so that the fifth fret matches the open A string.

Now reverse the process and play the A string at the fifth fret and adjust the pitch of the open D. Continue this process throughout the remainder of the strings:

Fret the D string at the fifth fret and tune the open G string to pitch.
Fret the G string at the fourth fret and tune the open B string.
Fret the B string at the fifth fret and tune the open high E string.

For more accuracy, let both notes ring together and tune with your right (picking) hand.

Fig. 4

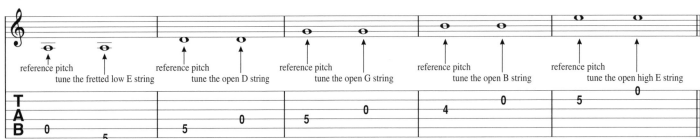

Tuning with Harmonics

Another popular tuning method involves *natural harmonics*. (A natural harmonic is the bell-like tone produced when an open string is plucked while a fret-hand finger lightly touches it above a designated fret location.) Strike the harmonic at the fifth fret of the low E string (lightly mute the string directly above the fret wire), let it ring, and strike the harmonic at the seventh fret of the A string. If they are out of tune, you'll hear a pulsation, or a series of "beats," as they're known. The faster the beat of the pulse the more out of tune the strings are. Assuming that your low E string is in tune, tune the A string (up or down) until the pulsation stops. This same fifth fret/seventh fret system applies to the A/D and D/G string sets. To tune the B string, hit the twelfth-fret harmonic on the G string and fret the B string at the eighth fret, then tune. Do this for the B and high E string set also, but fret the high E string at the seventh fret. (Note: This process offers a very close, but *approximate* tuning.)

Intonation

No amount of tuning will suffice if your guitar is not intonated properly. Intonation at the nut is best left to the hands of your local repairman, but bridge intonation in most cases is a do-it-yourself job. (If your bridge does not have adjustable saddles, this explanation won't work for you. In this case, visit your repairman.)

Start by putting on a new set of strings (many intonation problems are solved by this simple procedure) and tune them to pitch. The next step is to adjust the bridge saddle either forward or backward, until the twelfth-fret harmonic of each string (half-way point between the bridge and the nut) corresponds to the note fretted at the twelfth fret.

For example: Strike the twelfth-fret harmonic of the low E string and tune it to pitch (use an electronic tuner for this). Now, fret the low E string at the twelfth fret and check the tuning. If it's right on, there's no need to adjust the saddle. However, if it registers flat (lower), the string length (between bridge and nut) needs to be shortened. Do this by adjusting the bridge saddle forward (toward the neck) until the fretted note is in tune with the harmonic. If the note registers sharp (higher), the string needs to be lengthened. This is achieved by adjusting the bridge saddle back (away from the neck) until the fretted note is in tune. Follow the same procedure for each string.

If you still encounter tuning problems, here are a few troubleshooting tips:

- Make sure you aren't pressing too hard when you fret the strings. This can cause the strings to go sharp. (This problem is common with jumbo frets and guitars with scalloped fretboards.)

- Intonation may be off at the nut. In this case, it is wise to seek a good repairman.

- Always stretch your strings (pull up on each string, away from the fretboard) after tuning. This will take up any slack, which may accumulate at the tuning peg. After stretching the strings, repeat the tuning process.

CHAPTER 2: THEORY BASICS

Music notation is a system used to transcribe the three main components of music: *melody* (arrangement of pitches), *rhythm* (arrangement of pitches placed in time), and *harmony* (combination of two or more pitches).

MELODY

The Staff

Standard music notation is written on a grid consisting of five lines and four spaces, called a staff. The lines are counted from the bottom up (1–2–3–4–5), as are the spaces (1–2–3–4).

Fig. 1

At the beginning of every staff you'll find a symbol called a *clef*. There are many different types of clefs, but guitar music is notated on the *treble clef*, or *G clef* (Fig. 2).

Fig. 2

Each line and space of the staff is assigned a letter name. On the treble clef, the lines are (in order from bottom to top): E–G–B–D–F, as in "Every Good Boy Deserves Favor." The spaces are (in order from bottom to top): F–A–C–E, which of course spells "face."

Fig. 3

The Musical Alphabet

All pitches in music are assigned letter names. These letter names are the same as the first seven letters of the alphabet (A–B–C–D–E–F–G), and are referred to as the *musical alphabet*. Pitches are represented on the staff in the form of noteheads (circles and/or solid black dots). The higher the pitch, the higher it is placed on the staff. [Look again at the previous staff. Notice that if you line up the note names in order (line–space–line–space, etc.) from bottom to top, they follow the musical alphabet in sequential order: E–F–G–A–B–C–D–E–F.]

Many of the notes on the guitar fretboard extend beyond the staff. These pitches are notated using *ledger lines*—short lines that act as temporary staff extensions. (The only non-ledger-line notes that appear outside the staff are G, directly above the staff, and D, directly below the staff.) Check out Fig. 4 to see how they are used to represent some of the lowest and highest notes on the neck. (For an explanation of how tablature corresponds to the musical staff, refer to Fig. 20 in this chapter, and also the *Guitar Notation Legend* located at the back of the book.)

Notice that towards the end of Fig. 4 the notes drop back down and start climbing again. This is done when the ledger lines become too high and therefore impractical to read quickly. The notation "8va" indicates that these notes are to be played one octave higher than written. The use of 8va is left up to the discretion of the musical notator, but generally speaking the G note on the fourth ledger line is a good place to switch.

Fig. 4

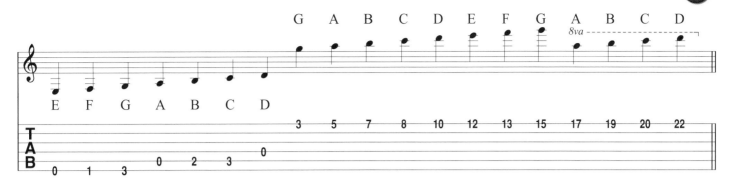

Accidentals

The musical alphabet consists of seven letters, but, as is clearly evident on the guitar fretboard, there are actually twelve possible tones. The five other pitches are named according to how they relate to their "natural-note" (A, B, C, D, E, F, G) neighbors. This note-naming process is achieved with the help of an *accidental* symbol. For instance, there is a note between A and B. This can either be named A# (spoken as *A sharp*), or B♭ (spoken as *B flat*). The "#" symbol raises the note by a half step (one fret), while the "♭" symbol lowers the note by a half step. (Refer to Fig. 1, Chapter 1, for an illustration of this process.)

There is a third accidental symbol called the *natural sign* (see Fig. 5 for accidental examples). The natural sign cancels previous sharps or flats, returning the note to its natural position. (Note: Accidentals always appear before the notehead in music notation.)

Fig. 5

Quiz #1

On the following quiz sheet (Fig. 6), fill in the note name above the staff, and the string/fret location on the tablature staff. You can refer to the neck diagram from Chapter 1, but try to do this by yourself. (With the exception of the high E string, the note locations don't go beyond the fourth fret.) To help get you started, the first few answers are included. When you're finished, check your answers in the "Answer Key" section located in the back of the book.

Fig. 6

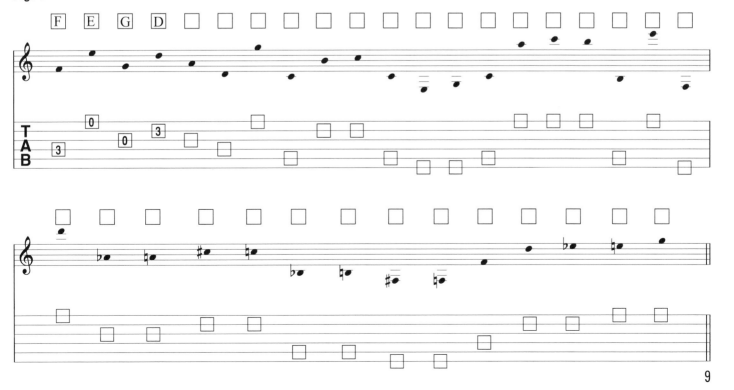

RHYTHM

Measures

As discussed, pitches are represented in vertical fashion (up and down) on the staff. Rhythms (pitches occurring in time) however, are represented in horizontal fashion along the staff, from left to right. To help keep track of rhythms and rests, the staff is divided into small segments called *measures*. Measures are separated by vertical slashes called *barlines*. A double barline (two thin lines) usually marks the end of a section. A terminal barline (the second line thicker and darker than the first) is used to mark the end of a piece of music.

Fig. 7

Time Signatures

At the beginning of a piece of guitar music (just to the right of the treble clef) is a pair of numbers, one on top of the other. This is called the *time signature.* The top number represents the number of beats (counts) per measure; the bottom number indicates the type of note receiving the beat. (See Fig. 8.) Sometimes the capital letter C is substituted in place of the time signature. This indicates common time, or 4/4 time.

Fig. 8

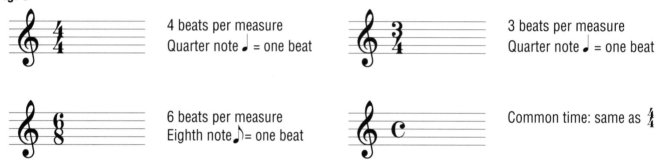

Note Values

As stated above, the location of a notehead on the staff indicates the pitch. The duration (or value) of the note, however, is indicated by the "shape" of the note. Fig. 9 offers a breakdown of the most common note values.

Fig. 9

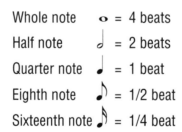

Rests

Rests indicate the length of silence between notes. Fig. 10 depicts the most common types of rests.

Fig. 10

Beams and Partial Beams

Notes that are less than one beat in value are often grouped together with the help of beams and/or partial beams (Fig. 11).

Fig. 11

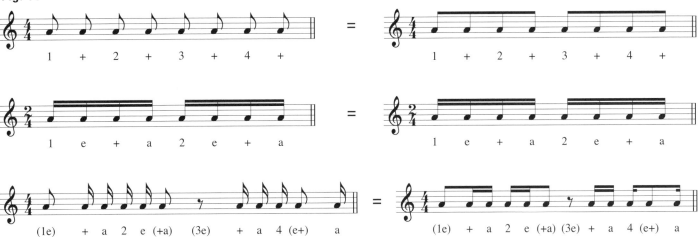

Triplets

A triplet is a group of three notes that occupies the same duration as two notes of the same value (Fig. 12).

Fig. 12

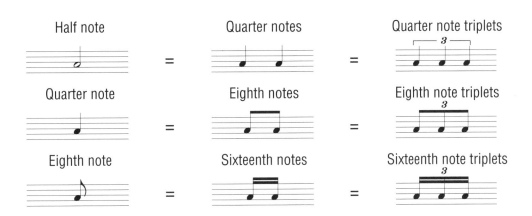

Dotted Notes

A dot (placed immediately after and parallel to the notehead) increases the value of that note (or rest) by one-half its original duration (Fig. 13).

Fig. 13

Ties

A tie is a curved line that connects two notes of the same pitch (not to be confused with a slur, which connects two notes of different pitch: refer to the *Guitar Notation Legend* for "slur"). A tie indicates that the two notes are treated as one, with the second one sustained as an extension of the first (Fig. 14).

Fig. 14

COUNT: 1   2   3   +   4   1   2   +   3   4   +   1   2   3   4   +   1   2   +   3   4

Quiz #2

On the following quiz sheet (Fig. 15), fill in the missing barlines in 4/4 time. For clues, refer to the topics covered in Figures 7–14. You'll find the answer key in the back of the book.

Fig. 15

HARMONY

In guitar music, harmony (two or more notes played at the same time) can be notated three different ways: 1) chord stacks (notes written on top of each other on the staff); 2) chord names (chord qualities written above the staff); and 3) chord frames (guitar neck diagrams depicting chord voicings).

Chord Stacks

Chord stacks are the traditional form of notating harmony. Following the same rules that apply to pitch notation, the notes are simply stacked on top of each other. (See Fig. 16.)

Fig. 16

Chord Names

Fig. 17 offers a more modern approach to notating guitar harmony. Here, the chord names (see Chord Construction, Chapter 7) are written above the staff, while the rhythms are notated with rhythm slashes (or hash marks) just below the chord names, or on the staff itself.

Fig. 17

Chord Frames

The third method for notating guitar harmony involves visual aids known as *chord frames*. Literally a snapshot of an isolated section of the fretboard (low E string on the left; high E string on the right), a chord frame uses dots to depict where notes are fretted, circles for open strings, Xs for muted strings, and a curved line to indicate a barre (two or more notes, on separate strings at the same fret, played with the same finger). Chord frames often include suggested fret-hand fingering written below the frame itself. When chord frames are used, rhythm slashes are generally written above the staff (see Fig. 18). (Note: The heavy line at the top of these chord frames represents the nut. If a voicing is to be played higher up the neck, a number to the right of the frame indicates the fret position: Ex: 8fr stands for eighth fret. See Fig. 19.)

Fig. 18

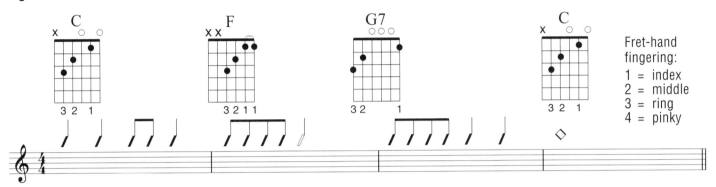

Fig. 19

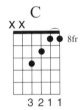

TABLATURE NOTATION

Tablature (*Tab* for short) is a graphic system that visually represents the guitar fretboard. Each horizontal line represents a string (bottom line is low E; top line is high E). Numbers are used to indicate where that string is to be fretted ("0" indicates an open string). In this book, tablature is written directly under the musical staff. Note: As the music staff contains the rhythmic information, there's no need to repeat it in the tablature staff (Fig. 20).

Fig. 20

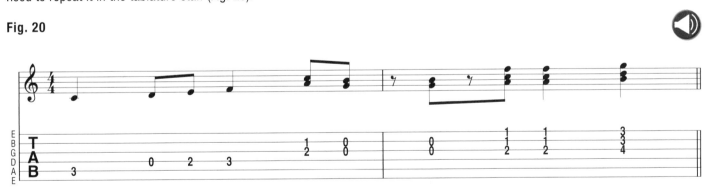

Tablature is an excellent system for indicating guitar nuances such as bends, slides, hammer-ons, pull-offs, and specific note placement in general. For a thorough explanation of tablature terms and symbols, refer to the *Guitar Notation Legend* located at the back of this book.

SHEET MUSIC AND CHART READING ROAD SIGNS

Before we close out this chapter, let's take a look at a few musical symbols used to navigate charts and sheet music.

Repeat Signs

Repeat signs are placed at the beginning and ending of a section which is to be replayed (Fig. 21).

Fig. 21

If the section is to be played more than twice, the amount of times is indicated above the repeat sign at the end of the section (Fig. 22).

Fig. 22

Play 4 times

First and Second Endings

First and second ending directions are written above the last measures of a section of music. The first ending appears just before the repeat signs and means to repeat the section, skip the first ending, then play the second ending (Fig. 23). [Note: Third and fourth endings (and beyond) are not uncommon occurrences.]

Fig. 23

D.C. and D.S.

The D.C. (Da Capo) sign means to return to the beginning and continue playing (Fig. 24).

Fig. 24

The D.S. (Dal Segno) sign means to return to the sign and continue playing (Fig. 25).

Fig. 25

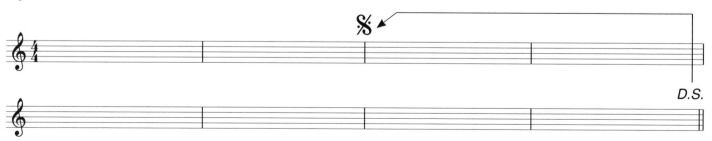

Al Coda

Often D.C. and D.S. instructions are accompanied with the term "al Coda" (to the coda). This means to follow the D.C. or D.S. instructions and when the "To Coda" sign is encountered, skip to the Coda (ending section). (Note: Always play through the "To Coda" sign the first time. In other words, you ignore the "To Coda" sign until the "D.S. al Coda" or "D.C. al Coda" signs instruct you to look for it.

Fig. 26

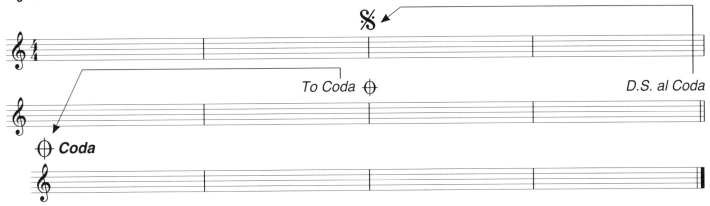

Tempo, Dynamics, and Other Markings

8va: Play an octave higher than written.

A tempo: Return to the original speed.

Accelerando: Gradually increase the tempo.

Accent (Fig. 27): Strike the note with more force than the surrounding notes.

Crescendo (Fig. 27): Gradually increase volume.

Decrescendo (Fig. 27): Gradually decrease volume.

f (forte): Loud.

ff (fortissimo): Very loud.

mf (mezzo forte): Medium loud.

mp (mezzo piano): Medium soft.

pp (pianissimo): Very soft.

p (piano): Soft.

Ritard: Gradually slow the tempo.

Rubato: Take liberties with the tempo.

Simile: Play in a similar fashion.

Staccato (Fig. 27): Play the note and quickly mute it.

Tacet: Don't play!

Tutti: Everyone plays the figure.

Fig. 27

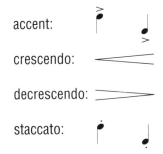

CHAPTER 3: SCALES AND KEY SIGNATURES

The major scale is the fundamental scale in Western music. In melodic terms, all traditional music theory is based on the major scale.

MAJOR SCALES

A *scale* is a succession of notes that are arranged in a specific order of intervals, from its tonic (root, or central note) to its octave. The *major* scale is a *diatonic* scale. That is to say it contains all seven notes of the musical alphabet. These notes of the scale are called *scale degrees* or *scale steps*. The *intervallic formula* (order of intervals) for the major scale goes as follows: whole step–whole step–half step–whole step–whole step–whole step–half step (W–W–H–W–W–W–H). (See Fig. 1).

Fig. 1

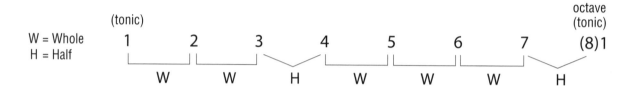

A great way to visualize the intervallic formula of the major scale is to play it along a single string. Fig. 2 lays the notes of the C major scale along the A string. As you play it, take note of the half-step locations between the 3rd and 4th degrees, and between the 7th and 8th (octave). Also, notice that the C major scale contains all natural notes (no sharps or flats).

Fig. 2

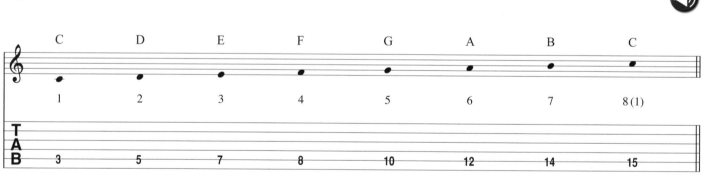

It's good to be able to play scales up and down a single string, but in practical terms, scales are learned in patterns that cross the neck in a vertical fashion. Fig. 3 lays out five patterns of the C major scale, as they appear up the neck, from *open position* (open strings and first three frets) to just beyond the twelfth fret. The root note (in this case, C) is circled in each pattern. (The additional pattern is the "fretted" version of the open-position pattern, an octave higher.)

Fig. 3

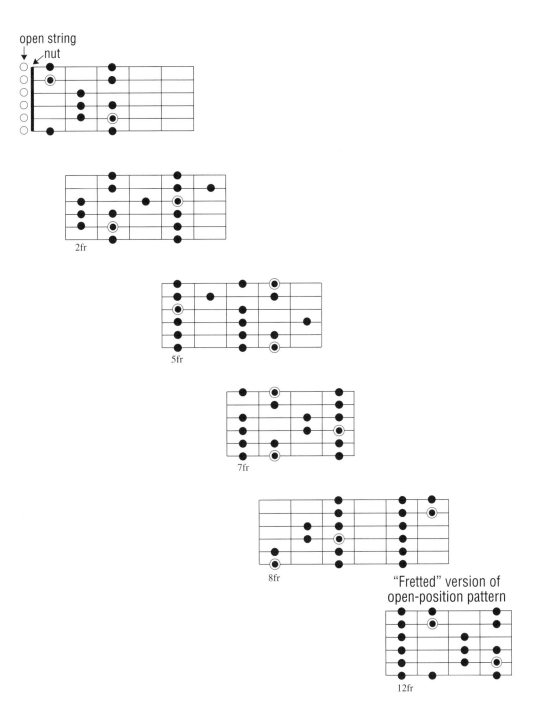

KEY SIGNATURES

The formula for the major scale remains the same regardless of the *key* (letter name of the tonic, or root) on which the scale is based. Taking into account that the C major scale contains all natural notes, this means that if a major scale starts on any note other than C, some (or all) of the notes need to be modified (raised or lowered) in order to fit the formula. For example, apply the major scale formula to the key of A (play along the A string, remembering to account for every letter name along the way), and you'll encounter three notes that fall between the cracks: C#, F#, and G# (Fig. 4).

Fig. 4

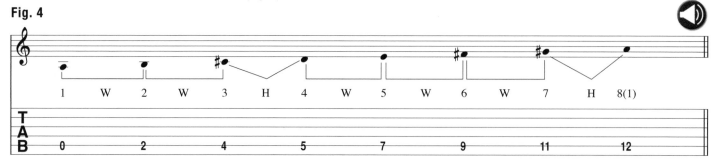

Now, play the B♭ major scale along the same string, and you'll encounter two oddball notes: B♭ (of course) and E♭ (Fig. 5).

Fig. 5

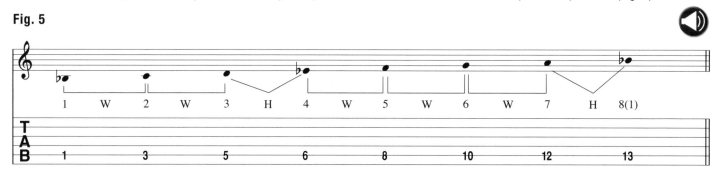

Judging by just these two examples, one would assume that a piece of music that wasn't in the key of C would be cluttered with an abundance of sharps or flats. This would be confusing indeed. What is needed is a system to organize accidentals. That system is called a key signature.

A *key signature* (placed on the staff just after the treble clef) indicates the notes that are to be raised or lowered throughout a piece of music. For example, we discovered that the A major scale calls for three notes to be raised a half step (C#, F#, and G#). Instead of writing a sharp sign before every one of those notes in a song though, those sharps are placed at the beginning of the music, in the key signature (Fig. 6).

Fig. 6

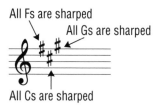

All Fs are sharped
All Gs are sharped
All Cs are sharped

Fig. 7 depicts all of the sharp key signatures, in order, from G to C#. (The key of C requires no key signature.)

Fig. 7

Just as there is an orderly system of sharp key signatures, there is one for flat keys (major scales which require certain notes to be lowered a half step). Fig. 8 displays these flat keys, in order, from the key of F, to the key of C♭.

Fig. 8

Circle of Fifths

In Fig. 9 you'll find a circular diagram called the circle of fifths. This handy device can be used to decipher many musical puzzles, among them the precise number and names of sharps or flats in any given major scale.

The "right" side of the circle (from G to F#) lists the keys containing sharps, while the "left" side (from F to G♭) lists the flat keys. The numbers along the inside of the circle indicate the number of sharps or flats in the corresponding key. (For example C contains no sharps or flats; D major contains 2 sharps; B♭ has 2 flats; and the keys of F# and G♭ contain 6 sharps and 6 flats, respectively.) The bracketed letters from F to B show the order of sharps as they appear on the staff. The bracketed letters from B♭ to G♭ show the order of flats. (After G♭, the order "jumps" back up to C and, finally, F.)

Fig. 9

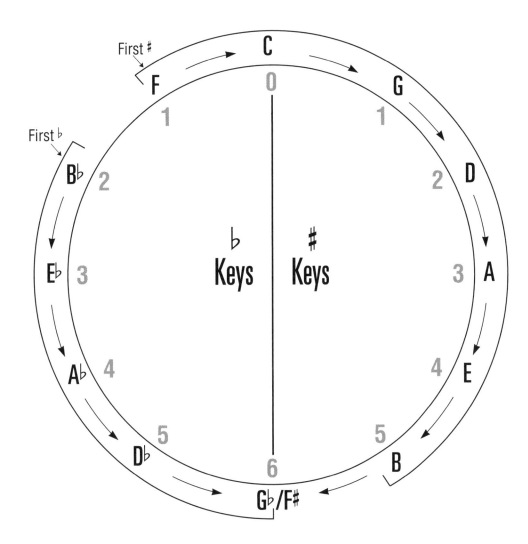

To get the most out of the circle of fifths, it's best to memorize it so you can visualize it in your mind's eye. A popular memorization tool is word association. For example, you could memorize the order of sharps by assigning a word to each letter name. Experts say "the sillier, the better," so here's one: **F**at **C**ats **G**o **D**own **A**lley **E**ndings **B**oldly **F**ighting. As for the order of flats, the first four letters spell "BEAD," so your formula could go something like this: **BEAD G**ames **C**ome **F**irst.

Here's an alternative, "hands on the guitar" approach to memorizing flat key signatures. Start with F on the first fret of the low E string and ascend in 4ths (refer to "Fretboard Layout" in Chapter 1) until you get to G♭ (Fig. 10). This gives you the order and names of the flat keys; after you get to G♭, just remember that C♭ (up a fourth) would be the last flat key.

Fig. 10

To memorize sharp key signatures, start on G on the third fret of the high E string and descend in 4ths until you arrive at F♯ on the low E string (Fig. 11). This gives you the order and names of the sharp keys (when you get to F♯, just remember that C♯ is the last sharp key).

Fig. 11

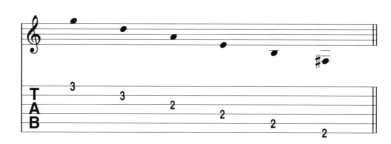

MINOR SCALES

For every major scale, there is a minor scale counterpart, or relative minor scale. ("Relative" means that the two scales share the same notes.) The relative minor scale is constructed by starting on the 6th degree of the major scale. For example, in Fig. 12 you'll find two octaves of the C major scale. Notice that the 6th degree is A. "Reassigning" the root of the C major scale to "A" creates the A minor scale (A–B–C–D–E–F–G). In other words, the A minor scale is constructed from the notes of the C major scale, starting on A.

Fig. 12

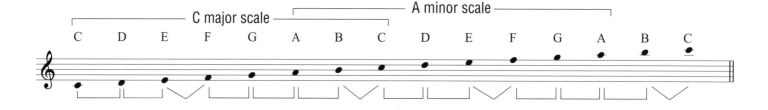

Notice that by starting from A instead of C, a different intervallic formula evolves: W–H–W–W–H–W–W. (Remember, the major scale is W–W–H–W–W–W–H.) This explains the melodic contrast of the two scales, even though they are related. As an experiment, play through the example in Fig. 13. Hear the difference? Even though the two scales share the same notes, they sound quite unalike.

Fig. 13

Here are five patterns of the A minor scale as they appear along the fretboard (Fig. 14). (Notice that, visually, they are the same as the C major scale patterns from Fig. 3. The only difference is the location of the roots. If you're confused, remember that the A minor scale and the C major scale are relative, meaning they are comprised of the same notes. This relativity is explored in depth in Chapter 11, "Modes.")

Fig. 14

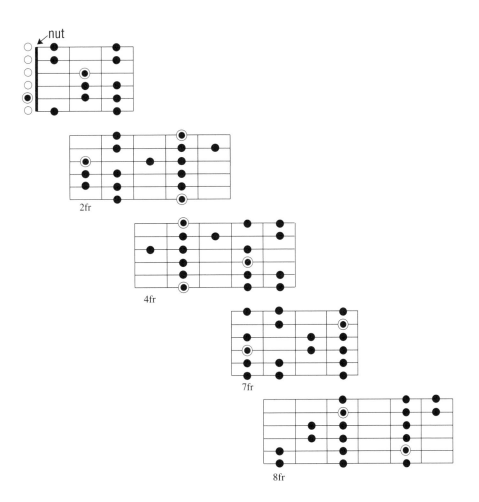

It's important to note that these, and the major scale patterns we saw earlier in Fig. 3, are movable to any key. Simply slide the selected pattern up or down the fretboard until the roots (circled notes) align with the desired tonic. (Example: The second A minor scale pattern placed at the fourth fret creates the B minor scale, because B is now the root.)

SCALE FORMULAS

A scale formula is a set of numbers used to describe a scale. Scale formulas allow for the identification of scales without having to refer to specific keys. As stated at the start of this chapter, a major portion of music theory is based on the major scale, and scale formulas are no exception.

The scale formula for the major scale is 1–2–3–4–5–6–7. These numbers correspond to the seven scale steps that make up the major scale. (The number "8" isn't included because it is simply the octave, where the scale starts over again.) These numbers also signify the intervallic formula of the major scale: W–W–H–W–W–W–H.

In Fig. 13 we discovered that the minor scale has a different intervallic formula from the major scale. This difference can be notated in the scale formula simply by adjusting the numbers. For example, take a look at Fig. 15.

Fig. 15

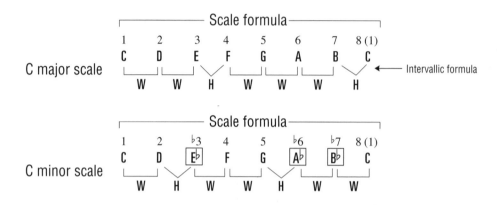

The first system depicts the notes of the C major scale, with the scale formula written above, and the intervallic formula written below. In the second system you'll find the notes of the C minor scale. Notice that the 1st, 2nd, 4th, and 5th scale steps (C, D, F, and G) are the same, but the others are different. This is because the intervallic structure of the minor scale is different, and causes a "shift" in the formula. This shift results in a lowering of the 3rd, 6th, and 7th degrees of the major scale by a half step. This half-step lowering is indicated in the scale formula with the use of flats: 1–2–♭3–4–5–♭6–♭7. This means that any major scale can be converted to a minor scale by lowering the 3rd, 6th, and 7th degrees by a half step.

MINOR KEY SIGNATURES

Minor key signatures correspond to their relative major key signatures. In other words, the D minor scale is relative to the F major scale, so the key signature for D minor is the same as F major: one flat (B♭). Fig. 16 provides a reference guide for minor key signatures.

Fig. 16

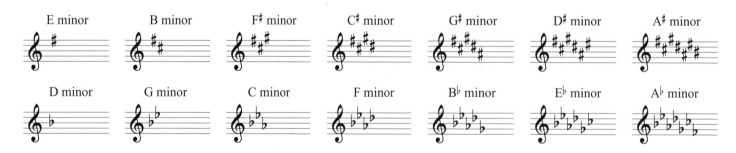

Quiz #3

On the following quiz (Fig. 17), you'll find a variety of major and minor scales written on the staff. All contain accidentals, which means they require a key signature. Your job is to figure out if the scale is major or minor, determine the key, and then fill in the proper key signature. (All the clues you'll need are found throughout this chapter.) Start by filling in the intervallic formula along the bottom of the staff. Next, write the corresponding scale formula along the top. Once you know if the scale is major or minor, fill in the proper key signature. The first three examples are completed, so you can use them as a guide.

Fig. 17

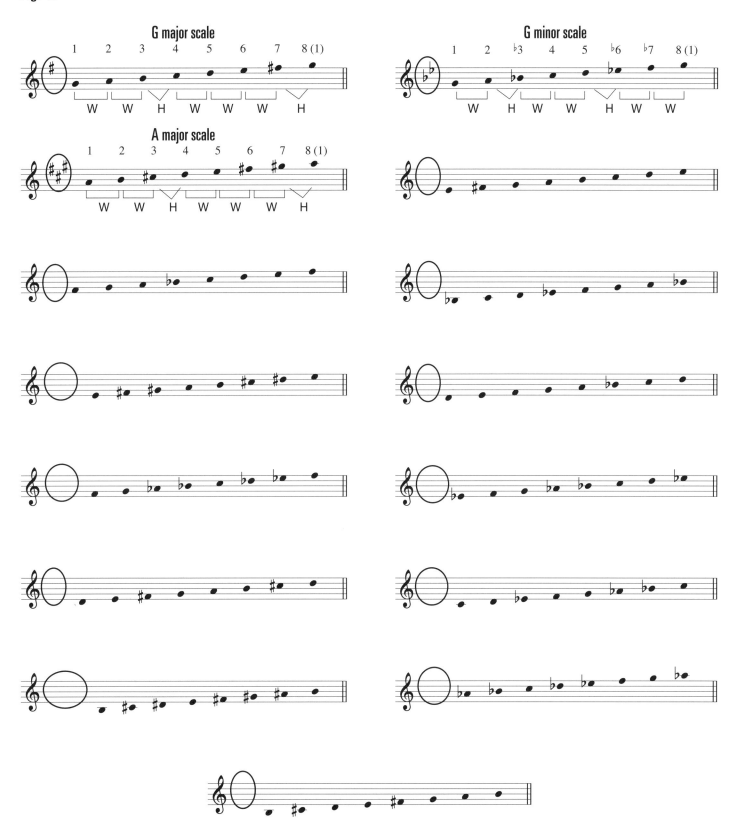

CHAPTER 4: INTERVALS

Intervals are the incremental building blocks from which melodies are constructed. This chapter provides an introduction to intervals and how to locate them on the fretboard.

INTERVAL NAMES

An *interval* is the distance between two notes. The smallest interval in Western music is the half step (the distance of one fret on the guitar). All intervals can be measured by the amount of half steps they contain, but the most common way to identify intervals is to refer to them by their proper names. The names of the intervals are based on the scale steps of the major scale. Take a look at Fig. 1.

Fig. 1

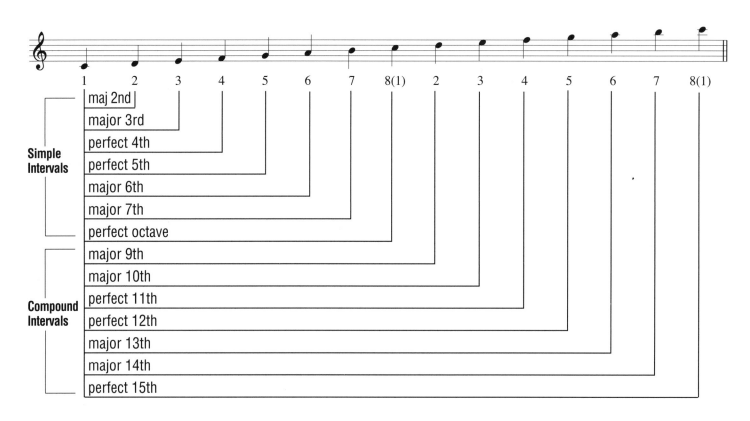

Written on the staff are two octaves of the C major scale, with the scale steps written above. The brackets below the staff measure the distance between the tonic and the other notes of the scale. Intervals within the first octave of the scale are called *simple intervals*. Notice that the names of these intervals directly correspond to the scale steps. For instance, the distance between the tonic and the second scale step is called a major 2nd; the distance between the tonic and the third step is called a major 3rd; etc. Once the octave is reached, higher numbers take over. These "beyond the octave" intervals are called *compound intervals*. In all cases, the number (2nd, 5th, 7th, etc.) describes the *interval quantity* (number of scale steps); and the adjective (major, minor, perfect, etc.) describes the *interval quality* (number of half steps).

Here is a reference list for the names of the intervals. (Note: Two half steps equals one whole step.)

Simple Intervals

0 steps = perfect unison (identical pitches)

1/2 step = minor 2nd

1 whole step = major 2nd

1 1/2 steps = minor 3rd

2 whole steps = major 3rd

2 1/2 steps = perfect 4th

3 whole steps = diminished 5th or tritone (augmented 4th)

3 1/2 steps = perfect 5th

4 whole steps = minor 6th (augmented 5th)

4 1/2 steps = major 6th (diminished 7th)

5 whole steps = minor 7th

5 1/2 steps = major 7th

6 whole steps = octave

Compound Intervals

octave + minor 2nd = minor 9th

octave + major 2nd = major 9th

octave + minor 3rd = augmented 9th

octave + major 3rd = major 10th

octave + perfect 4th = perfect 11th

octave + diminished 5th = diminished 12th/augmented 11th

octave + perfect 5th = perfect 12th

octave + minor 6th = minor 13th/augmented 12th

octave + major 6th = major 13th

octave + minor 7th = minor 14th

octave + major 7th = major 14th

two octaves = perfect 15th

INTERVAL FAMILIES

Intervals are grouped into two categories, or families: The major/minor family (2nds, 3rds, 6ths, and 7ths), and the perfect family (unisons, 4ths, 5ths, and octaves). When a major interval is lowered by a half step it is called *minor*. When a perfect interval is lowered by a half step it is called *diminished*. When a major or perfect interval is raised a half step it is called *augmented*. (See Fig. 2)

Fig. 2

Fig. 3 features a handy chart for deciphering the names of these "altered" intervals.

Fig. 3

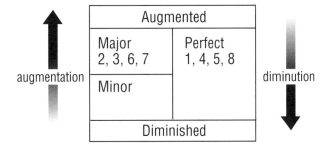

Augmented or diminished intervals, in certain keys, sometimes require a note to be raised or lowered twice (two half steps). These situations call for special accidentals known as double sharps and double flats (Fig. 4).

Fig. 4

INTERVAL SHAPES ON THE FRETBOARD

One of the most valuable (and overlooked) skills a guitarist can possess is the ability to recognize and play intervals on the fretboard. This becomes increasingly evident the more one grapples with mastering the instrument. Fig. 5 features interval shapes as they appear on the fretboard on the low string sets (low E and A; low E and D), with the lowest note on the sixth string. (Note: Whether ascending or descending, the name of the interval remains the same. In other words, either note can be considered the "root.") Treat this as a drill section, but try to commit as many as possible to memory.

Fig. 5

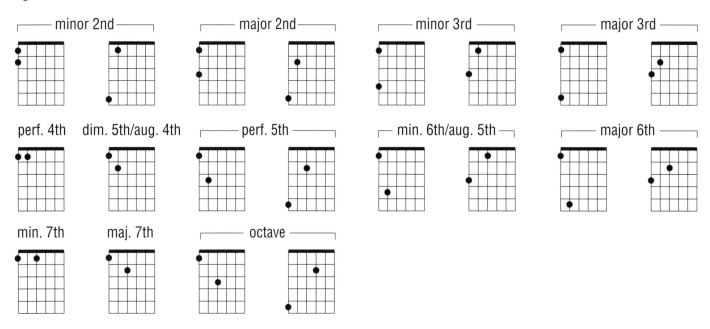

These shapes remain constant as you move to most other string sets (A and D; A and G; D and G; B and high E). But when the lower note of the interval is on the G string, or if the G string separates the two notes of an interval, the shape changes. This is due to the tuning of the guitar. (Remember that the strings are tuned in 4ths except for the third and second strings, which is a major 3rd.) Fig. 6 features these interval shapes.

Fig. 6

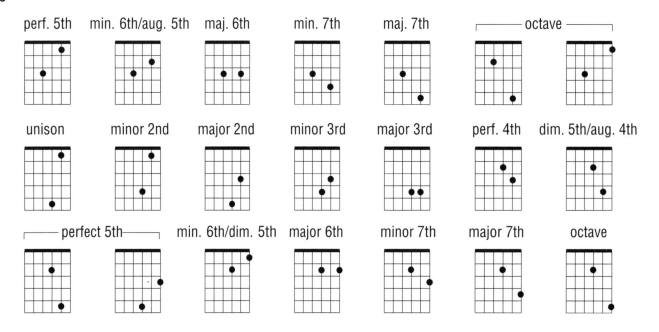

Committing all these interval shapes to memory may seem like a daunting task but it's well worth the effort. Here's a tip to help get you started: Learn the intervals on the lowest set of strings first (low E and A), then graduate to the higher sets.

MELODIC AND HARMONIC INTERVALS

When two notes are played one at a time, they form a *melodic interval*. When the two notes are played simultaneously, they form a *harmonic interval* (Fig. 7). In "guitar speak," harmonic intervals are usually referred to as *dyads*, or *double stops*, and sometimes, *couplets*.

Fig. 7

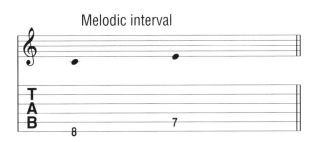
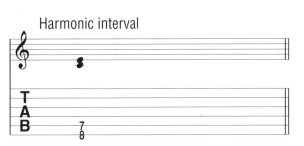

Quiz #4

On the following quiz (Fig. 8), fill in the correct interval name—both quantity and quality. Start by counting the number of lines and spaces between the notes. This discloses the number of scale steps, which determines the quantity. The difficult part is determining the quality. Use the reference list of intervals presented earlier in this chapter for help. You can also refer to the "interval shapes on the fretboard" from Figs. 5 & 6. Those shapes, used in conjunction with the fretboard diagram from Fig. 1 of Chapter 1, should help you find the answers.

Fig. 8

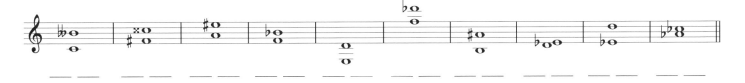

Here's a clue for determining interval qualities that don't have C as the bottom note. Assign the bottom note as the root of a major scale, and visualize its key signature. If the top note of the interval belongs to the scale (signified by the key signature), it's either major or perfect in quality. If the note lies outside the key signature (Fig. 9A), then the quality needs to be "adjusted." If you're already familiar with intervallic relationships within the C major scale, and you don't want to deal with key signatures, here's another approach: "Erase" any accidentals, determine the quality, then replace the accidental(s) and "adjust" the quality, if needed. (Fig. 9B)

Fig. 9A

Fig. 9B

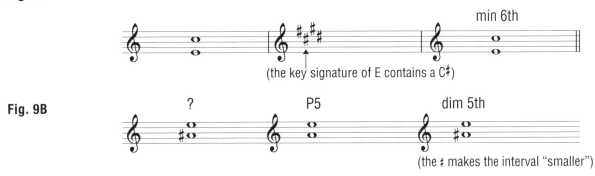

EAR TRAINING

A "good ear" is one of the most valuable assets a musician can possess. Some lucky people are born with "perfect pitch," but most musicians develop "relative pitch" (a sense of pitch which is based on comparisons) through ear training exercises.

Learning to recognize intervals "by ear" is a common, first-step approach to ear training. One popular method of interval training involves associating intervals with melodies and riffs from familiar songs. This is called *song association*. Here's a list of songs you can use to help you recognize simple ascending and descending intervals. (Except where indicated, the interval reflects the first two notes of the song.)

Ascending Intervals

Minor 2nd	Theme from "Jaws"
Major 2nd	"Frere Jacques"
Minor 3rd	"Greensleeves"
Major 3rd	"When the Saints Go Marching In"
Perfect 4th	"Here Comes the Bride"
Diminished 5th	Theme from "The Simpsons"
Perfect 5th	"2001: A Space Odyssey"
Minor 6th	Opening riff of "Fortunate Son" (CCR)
Major 6th	Opening riff of "Soul Man"
Minor 7th	"Star Trek" (original television theme)
Major 7th	1st and 3rd vocal notes of "Immigrant Song"
Octave	"Somewhere Over the Rainbow"

Descending Intervals

Minor 2nd	Theme from "Jurassic Park"
Major 2nd	"Three Blind Mice"
Minor 3rd	"Hey Jude"
Major 3rd	"Summertime"
Perfect 4th	"The Wave" (7th Inning Stretch)
Diminished 5th	Opening notes of "Red House" (Jimi Hendrix)
Perfect 5th	Theme from "The Flintstones"
Minor 6th	Theme from "Love Story"
Major 6th	"Nobody Knows the Trouble I've Seen"
Minor 7th	Riff of "Man in the Box" - harmonic interval
Major 7th	1st and 3rd notes of "I Love You" (Cole Porter)
Octave	Main riff of "Jump, Jive and Wail"

Traditional ear training drills involve recognizing musical materials and notating them on the staff without the aid of an instrument. In this drill however, you are required to actually *play* what you hear. In each audio example you will hear two notes played separately (melodic interval) and then simultaneously (harmonic interval). Your job is to recognize the interval, and then play it on the guitar. This will strengthen your ear as well as help you to visualize intervallic shapes on the fretboard. (Once you've identified the interval and played it on the guitar, jot down the answer in the space provided.) The bottom note in each example will always be C, played on the low E string at the 8th fret. To help get you started, the first five examples are transcribed in Fig. 10.

Fig. 10

The next set of examples includes minor 2nds, major 2nds, minor 3rds, and major 3rds (Fig. 11). You can check your results in the Answer Key, located at the back of the book.

Fig. 11

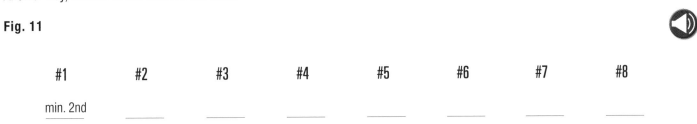

The following examples include perfect 4ths, perfect 5ths, octaves, and diminished 5ths (Fig. 12).

Fig. 12

The last set of examples includes minor 6ths, major 6ths, minor 7ths, and major 7ths (Fig. 13).

Fig. 13

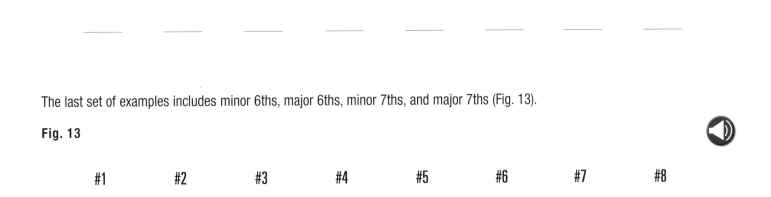

CHAPTER 5: TRIADS

As we learned in the last chapter, two notes played together form a *harmonic interval*, the smallest unit of harmony. Three or more tones played simultaneously form a chord. The most common, basic chords are made up of specific arrangements of three notes, which are a 3rd interval (major or minor) apart. These three-note chords are called *triads*. A firm understanding of triads is essential for comprehending more complex chord types and progressions.

MAJOR AND MINOR TRIADS

Major and minor triads are the most common, fundamental chords: common because they are found in virtually all styles of music, and fundamental in that they are *the* determining factors when categorizing more complex chords.

The *major triad* is constructed from the root, 3rd, and 5th of the major scale. Fig. 1 depicts this process using our old friend, the C major scale.

Fig. 1

Just as scales have formulas, so do triads. The formula for the major triad is 1–3–5. This relates to the major scale of course, and translates as such: from the root to the 3rd is a major 3rd; from the root to the 5th is a perfect 5th. It's also important to note the distance between the 3rd and 5th, which is a minor 3rd.

This in mind, a major triad can be constructed from any note by stacking a major 3rd interval, followed by a minor 3rd interval. This is an important revelation for visualizing triads on the neck. Fig. 2 offers some examples of major triad shapes on the fretboard.

Fig. 2

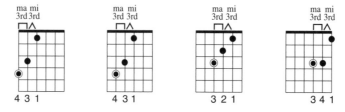

The *minor triad* construction is the same as its major counterpart, except that the 3rd is lowered by a half step. Fig. 3 shows this conversion process applied to C, D, and E♭ major triads.

Fig. 3

Just as the major scale formula is the template for describing all scales, so is the major triad formula for describing triads. In other words, a minor triad is described by how it relates to a major triad: 1–♭3–5. It's important to note that, although the distance between the root and the 5th is the same (perfect 5th), the lowering of the 3rd changes the "stacked" interval structure. Whereas the intervallic makeup of a major triad is major 3rd–minor 3rd, a minor triad is minor 3rd–major 3rd. Again, this is an important concept when it comes to transferring triads from the staff onto the fretboard (Fig. 4).

Fig. 4

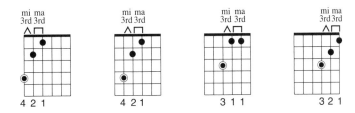

AUGMENTED AND DIMINISHED TRIADS

In addition to major and minor, there are two other types of triads: augmented and diminished. Though they are encountered much less frequently, they are important for understanding the structure of more complex chords.

An *augmented* triad is a major triad with a raised 5th: 1–3–♯5, as in C–E–G♯ (Fig. 5). Notice the interval structure is major 3rd–major 3rd.

Fig. 5

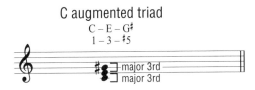

Fig. 6 offers some voicings of augmented triads.

Fig. 6

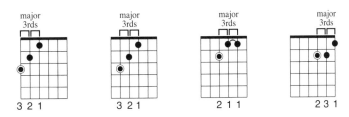

A *diminished* triad is a minor triad with a lowered 5th: 1–♭3–♭5, as in C–E♭–G♭ (Fig. 7).

Fig. 7

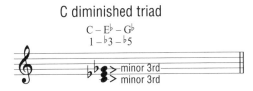

Fig. 8 offers some voicings of diminished triads.

Fig. 8

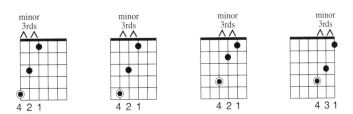

Why are there only four triads? Because there are only four possible combinations of two superimposed (stacked) 3rd intervals: major–minor (major triad); minor–major (minor triad); major–major (augmented triad); and minor–minor (diminished triad). Use these four formulas to help you name the triads in the following quiz (Fig. 9). (Answers are in the back of the book.)

Fig. 9

INVERSIONS

Triads don't always appear in an orderly, root–3rd–5th fashion. Quite the contrary, they can be voiced in a variety of combinations. Let's take a look at a few examples.

In Fig. 10 you'll find three triads. The first is a C major triad in *root position*, which means the "root" (C) is in the bass. The second places the root on top, so that the 3rd is in the bass. The last one places the 5th in the bass. The notes of the triad are still the same (C, E, and G), but they've just been placed in a different vertical order.

Fig. 10

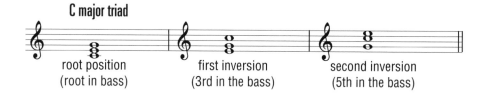

These last two triads are called *inverted triads*. An inverted triad is a triad that has its 3rd or 5th in the bass, rather than its root. When the 3rd is in the bass, it's called *first inversion*. When the 5th is in the bass, it's called *second inversion*. Check out Fig. 11 for inverted major and minor triads shapes as they appear on the fretboard. Remember, these can be transposed to any key.

Fig. 11

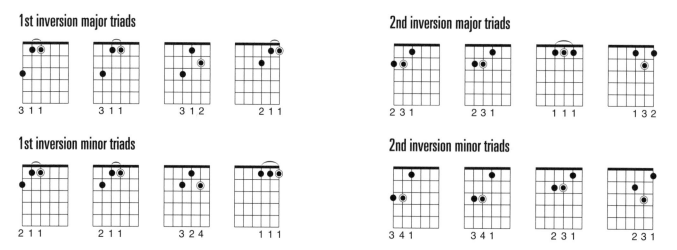

OPEN TRIADS

Triads can also be voiced with their notes spread very far apart. These types of triads are called *open triads*. In an open triad, the notes span more than one octave, as opposed to the *closed* triads with which we began. Fig. 12 depicts a variety of open triads, both on the staff and on chord frames. Note that some of these triads are inverted as well. The E minor is in first inversion; the D major is in second inversion, etc.

Fig. 12

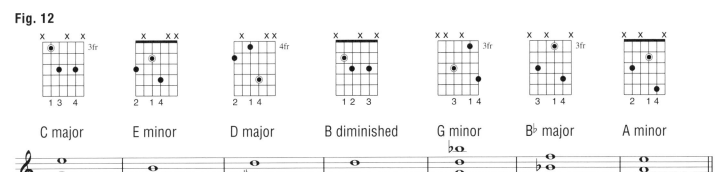

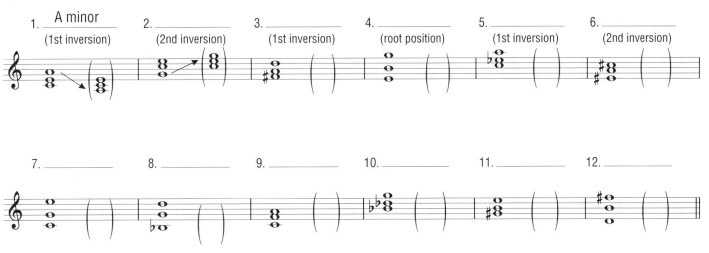

Quiz #6

Rearrange the notes of the following inverted and open triads (Fig. 13) until they are stacked in 3rd intervals (as close as possible). Then write in the proper name. Some examples include helpful hints, while others don't. (Answers are in the back of the book.)

Fig. 13

Ear Training Drill #2

This ear training drill is in three parts: 1) Recognizing root-position major, minor, augmented, and diminished triads; 2) inverted major and minor triads; and 3) open major and minor triads. In each example, the lowest note of the triad is sounded, followed by the entire triad, and finally, the notes of the triad played one at a time (arpeggiated). Write your answers in the blanks provided in Figs. 14A–14C.

Before you start, consider these sonic characteristics of triads: Major and minor triads are considered *consonant* (smooth sounding; pleasing; stable; restful; etc.). Major triads tend to have a happy, pretty quality, while minor triads sound sad, wistful, and bittersweet. Augmented and diminished triads are *dissonant* (tense; disturbing; anxious; etc.). Augmented triads have a slightly brighter quality compared to the darker sound of diminished triads.

Fig. 14A

#1   #2   #3   #4   #5   #6   #7   #8   #9   #10   #11   #12

____   ____   ____   ____   ____   ____   ____   ____   ____   ____   ____   ____

Fig. 14B

#1   #2   #3   #4   #5   #6   #7   #8   #9   #10   #11   #12

____   ____   ____   ____   ____   ____   ____   ____   ____   ____   ____   ____

Fig. 14C

#1   #2   #3   #4   #5   #6   #7   #8   #9   #10   #11   #12

____   ____   ____   ____   ____   ____   ____   ____   ____   ____   ____   ____

CHAPTER 6: HARMONIZING THE MAJOR SCALE

The theory of chord construction and chord progressions is steeped in a process known as *harmonizing the major scale*—a system in which chords are constructed by stacking the notes of the major scale in 3rds. This harmonization process is also referred to as diatonic harmony.

DIATONIC TRIADS

Let's start by harmonizing the C major scale in triads. The first step is to write out the scale on the staff (Fig. 1A). Next, place the note that is a diatonic 3rd interval higher (two notes away in the same scale), above each scale step (Fig. 1B). The scale is now harmonized in 3rds. (Notice that some are major, while others are minor.) Finally, place the note that is a diatonic 3rd away on top of the second note (Fig. 1C). Now the process is complete: the C major scale harmonized in triads.

Fig. 1A

C major scale

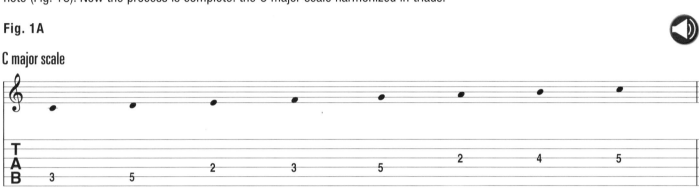

Fig. 1B

Harmonized in 3rds

Fig. 1C

Harmonized in triads

The triad qualities are notated below the staff. (The actual chord names are written above.) This is the triad formula for the major scale, and it never deviates, no matter what key: major–minor–minor–major–major–minor–diminished. Commit it to memory, as it is the foundation for many songs and chord progressions.

Roman Numeral Notation

As discussed in Chapter 3, Arabic numbers (1, 2, 3, etc.) are used to describe scale steps. Chords, however, are identified with Roman numerals (I, II, III, etc.), both uppercase (I) and lowercase (iii). Roman numerals describe a chord's quality and *function*, or how it relates to the key of the progression. An uppercase Roman numeral indicates a major triad, lowercase represents a minor triad, and the numeric value reflects the root of the chord as it corresponds to the scale degree. A small circle (°) placed after a chord name or lowercase Roman numeral indicates a diminished triad. According to this system, the formula for harmonized triads of the major scale reads: I–ii–iii–IV–V–vi–vii° (Fig. 2).

Fig. 2

I	ii	iii	IV	V	vi	vii°
C	Dm	Em	F	G	Am	B°

If you know the key signature of every key, it's relatively simple to harmonize any major scale. Start by writing out the names of the notes of the scale, and then simply add the appropriate chord quality to each scale step. Fig. 3 offers a handy chart for reference.

Fig. 3

Harmonized Major Scales (Triads)

Key	I	ii	iii	IV	V	vi	vii°
C	C	Dm	Em	F	G	Am	B°
G	G	Am	Bm	C	D	Em	F♯°
D	D	Em	F♯m	G	A	Bm	C♯°
A	A	Bm	C♯m	D	E	F♯m	G♯°
E	E	F♯m	G♯m	A	B	C♯m	D♯°
B	B	C♯m	D♯m	E	F♯	G♯m	A♯°
G♭	G♭	A♭m	B♭m	C♭	D♭	E♭m	F°
D♭	D♭	E♭m	Fm	G♭	A♭	B♭m	C°
A♭	A♭	B♭m	Cm	D♭	E♭	Fm	G°
E♭	E♭	Fm	Gm	A♭	B♭	Cm	D°
B♭	B♭	Cm	Dm	E♭	F	Gm	A°
F	F	Gm	Am	B♭	C	Dm	E°

DIATONIC SEVENTH CHORDS

Triads are the most fundamental of all chords and form the basis for many popular songs—especially in rock, folk, and country. In styles such as jazz, funk, and blues, however, it is customary to employ more complex, colorful chords known as *seventh chords.*

A seventh chord is a combination of a triad with an added interval of a 7th. This translates to a triad with another 3rd interval placed on top. In Fig. 4A you'll find the C major scale harmonized in triads. Fig. 4B stacks another diatonic 3rd interval above each triad. This also translates to a diatonic 7th interval from the root of each triad. The result is the C major scale harmonized in seventh chords. You'll notice that these chords contain some pretty serious stretches in the left hand. For this reason, seventh chords are rarely voiced in a closed manner. We'll see more on their voicing later.

Figs. 4A–4B

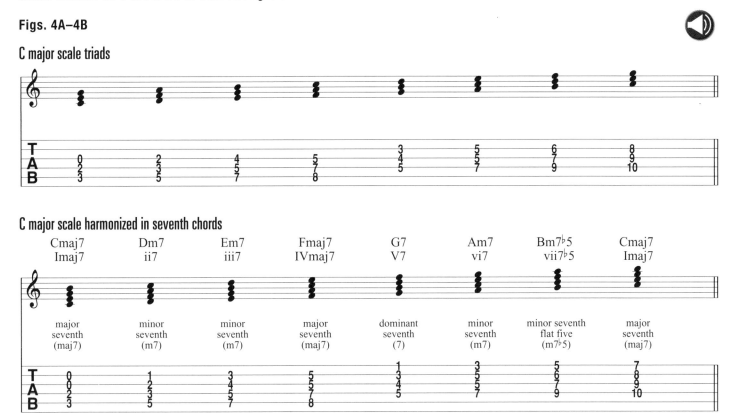

Now, compare these seventh chords to the triads in Fig. 1C:

- The I and IV major triads now have added major 7th intervals above their roots (B and E, respectively). Major triads with major 7ths attached (1–3–5–7) are called *major seventh chords* (Cmaj7 and Fmaj7; Imaj7 and IVmaj7).

- The ii, iii, and vi minor triads now have added minor 7th intervals (C, D, and G, respectively). Minor triads with minor 7ths attached (1–♭3–5–♭7) are called *minor seventh chords* (Dm7, Em7, and Am7; ii7, iii7, and vi7).

- The V major triad also has an added minor 7th interval (F). A major triad with a minor 7th (1–3–5–♭7) is called a *dominant seventh chord* (G7; V7).

- The vii° triad now has an added minor 7th interval (A). A diminished triad with a minor 7th (1–♭3–♭5–♭7) is called a *minor seven flat-five chord*, or *half diminished* (Bm7♭5; vii7♭5).

(Note: Here's a short-cut method for decoding major and minor 7th intervals: Transpose the interval an octave down, so that it is below the root. If it is a half step below, it's a major 7th. If it's a whole step below, it's a minor 7th.)

After you've memorized the triad formula for the major scale, memorize the seventh-chord formula as well: Imaj7–ii7–iii7–IVmaj7–V7–vi7–vii7♭5. Once you know the formula, it's easy to harmonize any major scale. Simply write down each scale step, and attach the appropriate quality. Use the chart in Fig. 5 (on the following page) for reference.

Fig. 5

Harmonized Major Scales (Seventh Chords)

Key	Imaj7	ii7	iii7	IVmaj7	V7	vi7	vii7♭5
C	Cmaj7	Dm7	Em7	Fmaj7	G7	Am7	Bm7♭5
G	Gmaj7	Am7	Bm7	Cmaj7	D7	Em7	F♯m7♭5
D	Dmaj7	Em7	F♯m7	Gmaj7	A7	Bm7	C♯m7♭5
A	Amaj7	Bm7	C♯m7	Dmaj7	E7	F♯m7	G♯m7♭5
E	Emaj7	F♯m7	G♯m7	Amaj7	B7	C♯m7	D♯m7♭5
B	Bmaj7	C♯m7	D♯m7	Emaj7	F♯7	G♯m7	A♯m7♭5
G♭	G♭maj7	A♭m7	B♭m7	C♭maj7	D♭7	E♭m7	Fm7♭5
D♭	D♭maj7	E♭m7	Fm7	G♭maj7	A♭7	B♭m7	Cm7♭5
A♭	A♭maj7	B♭m7	Cm7	D♭maj7	E♭7	Fm7	Gm7♭5
E♭	E♭maj7	Fm7	Gm7	A♭maj7	B♭7	Cm7	Dm7♭5
B♭	B♭maj7	Cm7	Dm7	E♭maj7	F7	Gm7	Am7♭5
F	Fmaj7	Gm7	Am7	B♭maj7	C7	Dm7	Em7♭5

In order to fully grasp deeper, more complex harmonic concepts, it's important to view the intervallic makeup of seventh chords from all angles.

- Major seventh chords: From the root to the 3rd is a major 3rd; from the 3rd to the 5th is a minor 3rd; from the 5th to the 7th is a major 3rd; from the root to the 5th is a perfect 5th; and from the root to the 7th is a major 7th.

- Minor seventh chords: From the root to the 3rd is a minor 3rd; from the 3rd to the 5th is a major 3rd; from the 5th to the 7th is a minor 3rd; from the root to the 5th is a perfect 5th; and from the root to the 7th is a minor 7th.

- Dominant seventh chords: From the root to the 3rd is a major 3rd; from the 3rd to the 5th is a minor 3rd; from the 5th to the 7th is a minor 3rd; from the root to the 5th is a perfect 5th; and from the root to the 7th is a minor 7th.

- Minor seventh flat-five chords: From the root to the 3rd is a minor 3rd; from the 3rd to the 5th is a minor 3rd; from the 5th to the 7th is a major 3rd; from the root to the 5th is a diminished 5th; and from the root to the 7th is a minor 7th.

Once you're familiar with major scale harmony, start drilling yourself in the following manner:

What are the I, IV, and V triads of F major? Answer: F, B♭, and C.

What is iim7–V7–Imaj7 in D major? Answer: Em7–A7–Dmaj7.

What is the V chord of E? Answer: B.

What is the V7 chord of B♭? Answer: F7.

What is I–vi–IV–V in G major? Answer: G–Em–C–D.

Quiz #7

(Answers are in the back of the book.)

1) What is a major triad with a minor seventh? _____

2) What is a minor triad with a minor seventh? _____

3) What is a diminished triad with a minor seventh? _____

4) What is a major triad with a major seventh? _____

5) What is the V7 chord of E major? _____

6) What is the quality of the ii, iii, and vi chords in seventh chord form? _____

7) What is the vii° triad in A♭ major? _____

8) What are the I, IV, and V triads in G major? ___ ___ ___

9) What are the I, IV, and V seventh chords in A major? ___ ___ ___

10) What are the I, vi, IV, and V triads in F major? ___ ___ ___ ___

11) What is the iii chord (seventh chord form) of B♭ major? _____

12) What is the vi chord (seventh chord form) of E major? _____

CHAPTER 7: CHORD CONSTRUCTION

This chapter is a study in chord construction—both in theory, and on the fretboard.

MAJOR AND MINOR CHORDS

The technical definition of a chord is three or more notes played together at the same time. The most common, fundamental chords are major and minor chords.

A *major chord* is simply an arrangement of the notes in a major triad (1–3–5). How these notes are arranged determines the chord's *voicing*, or how it appears on the fretboard. Fig. 1 offers several voicings of a C major chord. Notice that some of the chord tones (notes of the chord) are doubled (or even tripled), but in all cases, every note of the chord is represented at least once. Also notice that even when the root is not in the bass (as in first and second inversion), it's still considered a C major chord. The root note (C) has been circled.

Fig. 1

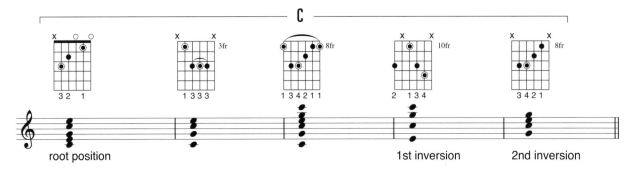

The chord voicings that don't contain open strings are movable to any key. Simply slide the voicing up or down the fretboard until the circled note (root) aligns with the root of the chord you wish to play. For example, the third voicing placed at the third fret would be a G chord; at the fifth fret it would be an A chord.

A *minor chord* consists of the notes in a minor triad (1–♭3–5) arranged in any combination. Fig. 2 offers several voicings of a C minor (Cm) chord.

Fig. 2

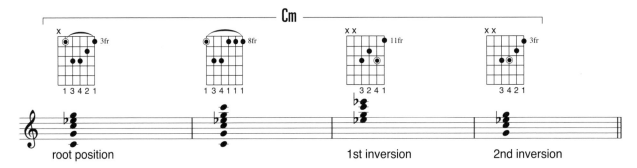

The *major chord* is the only chord that doesn't require a suffix—a symbol that indicates the chord type, or quality. For instance, E♭ means E♭ major. E♭ with an added suffix means that E♭ is still the root, but the quality is something other than major. There are many different types of chords, so there are a great many suffixes. The chart below includes suffixes and brief explanations of what they mean. (They all have C as their roots). Use it as a reference guide as you read through the chapter.

Symbol	Chord Type	Formula	Note Names
C	C major	1–3–5	C–E–G
Cm	C minor	1–♭3–5	C–E♭–G
C5	C power chord	1–5	C–G
C+	C augmented	1–3–♯5	C–E–G♯
C°	C diminished	1–♭3–♭5	C–E♭–G♭
Csus4	C suspended 4th	1–4–5	C–F–G
Csus2	C suspended 2nd	1–2–5	C–D–G
Cadd9	C major w/ added 9th	1–3–5–9	C–E–G–D
Cm(add9)	C minor w/ added 9th	1–♭3–5–9	C–E♭–G–D
C6	C major w/ added 6th	1–3–5–6	C–E–G–A
Cm6	C minor with added 6th	1–♭3–5–6	C–E♭–G–A
C6/9	C major w/ added 6th & 9th	1–3–5–6–9	C–E–G–A–D
Cm6/9	C minor w/ added 6th & 9th	1–♭3–5–6–9	C–E♭–G–A–D
Cmaj7	C major seventh	1–3–5–7	C–E–G–B
Cm7	C minor seventh	1–♭3–5–♭7	C–E♭–G–B♭
C7	C dominant seventh	1–3–5–♭7	C–E–G–B♭
Cm7♭5	C minor seventh flat five	1–♭3–♭5–♭7	C–E♭–G♭–B♭
C°7	C diminished seventh	1–♭3–♭5–♭♭7	C–E♭–G♭–B♭♭
C7sus4	C seventh suspended 4th	1–4–5–♭7	C–F–G–B♭
Cm(maj7)	C minor major seventh	1–♭3–5–7	C–E♭–G–B
Cmaj9	C major ninth	1–3–5–7–9	C–E–G–B–D
Cm9	C minor ninth	1–♭3–5–♭7–9	C–E♭–G–B♭–D
C9	C dominant ninth	1–3–5–♭7–9	C–E–G–B♭–D
C9sus4	C ninth suspended 4th	1–4–5–♭7–9	C–F–G–B♭–D
Cm11	C minor eleventh	1–♭3–5–♭7–9–11	C–E♭–G–B♭–D–F
C11	C eleventh	1–3–5–♭7–9–11	C–E–G–B♭–D–F
Cmaj13	C major thirteenth	1–3–5–7–9–13	C–E–G–B–D–A
Cm13	C minor thirteenth	1–♭3–5–♭7–9–11–13	C–E♭–G–B♭–D–F–A
C13	C thirteenth	1–3–5–♭7–9–13	C–E–G–B♭–D–A
(Altered Chords)			
Cmaj7♭5	C major seventh flat five	1–3–♭5–7	C–E–G♭–B
Cmaj7♯11	C major seventh sharp eleven	1–3–5–7–♯11	C–E–G–B–F♯
C+7	C augmented seventh	1–3–♯5–♭7	C–E–G♯–B♭
C7♭5	C seventh flat five	1–3–♭5–♭7	C–E–G♭–B♭
C7♭9	C seventh flat nine	1–3–5–♭7–♭9	C–E–G–B♭–D♭
C7♯9	C seventh sharp nine	1–3–5–♭7–♯9	C–E–G–B♭–D♯
C7♭9♯5	C augmented seventh flat nine	1–3–♯5–♭7–♭9	C–E–G♯–B♭–D♭
C7♯9♯5	C augmented seventh sharp nine	1–3–♯5–♭7–♯9	C–E–G♯–B♭–D♯
C13♭9	C thirteenth flat nine	1–3–5–♭7–♭9–13	C–E–G–B♭–D♭–A
C13♯9	C thirteenth sharp nine	1–3–5–♭7–♯9–13	C–E–G–B♭–D♯–A

SUSPENDED CHORDS, POWER CHORDS, AND "ADD" CHORDS

A suspended second chord (sus2) can be viewed as either a major or minor chord with its 3rd replaced with a major second (1–2–5). The result is an ambiguous-sounding chord that can be used when neither a major nor minor tonality is strongly desired. See Fig. 3 for some Asus2 voicings.

Fig. 3

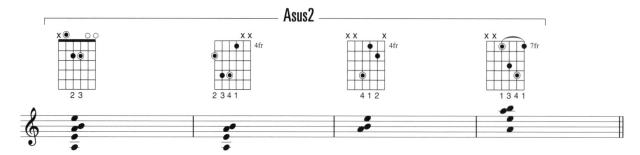

A suspended fourth chord (sus4) is similar to a sus2, except that a perfect 4th acts as the suspended note (1–4–5). These chords often "resolve" to a parallel (same root) major or minor chord. For example, an Esus4 might resolve to either an E or an Em chord. Fig. 4 features Esus4 voicings.

Fig. 4

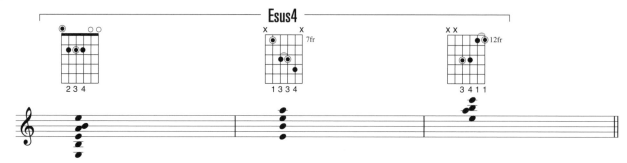

Power chords (root/5th chords) are the exception to the "three notes make a chord" rule, because they only contain two notes: a root and a 5th. They are perennial fixtures in rock music and are generally voiced on the lower string sets (Fig. 5). The suffix for a power chord is the number "5."

Fig. 5

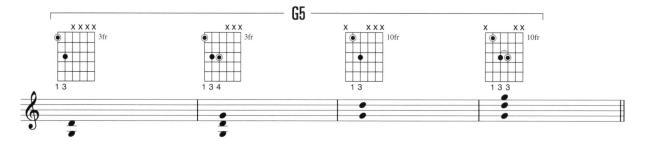

The suffix "add" means to insert a note that is not included in the chord voicing. Add chords are often major or minor chords with an added 9th (1–3–5–9 & 1–♭3–5–9) as in Aadd9 and Am(add9) (Fig. 6A). Add4 chords are also widespread in modern pop music. These are major and minor chords with an added 4th (1–3–4–5 and 1–♭3–4–5) as in Dadd4 and Bm(add4) (Fig. 6B).

Fig. 6A–6B

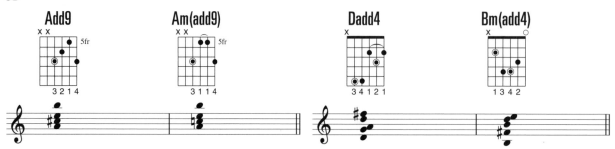

SIXTH CHORDS AND SIX/NINE CHORDS

Sixth chords are major or minor chords with an added major 6th degree (1–3–5–6 or 1–♭3–5–6). (A common mistake is to add a minor 6th to a minor sixth chord.) They have a jazzy sound and work great in jazz and blues (Fig. 7). Notice that the eighth-position chords omit the 5th degree. Omitting the 5th is common practice with guitar voicings. In most cases, this doesn't have any impact on the naming of the chord.

Fig. 7

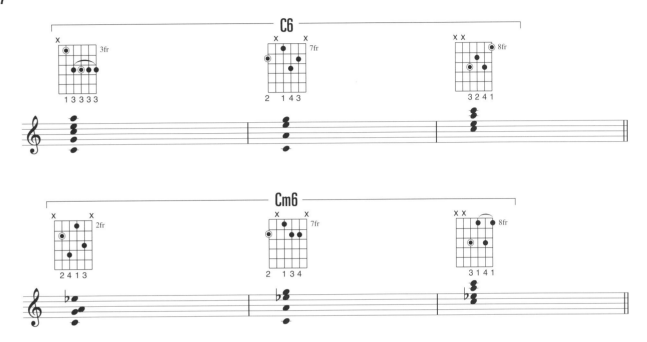

Six/nine chords are major or minor chords with an added 6th and 9th (1–3–5–6–9 and 1–♭3–5–6–9). Quite common in Latin, they have a pretty sound and work great for ending chords (Fig. 8).

Fig. 8

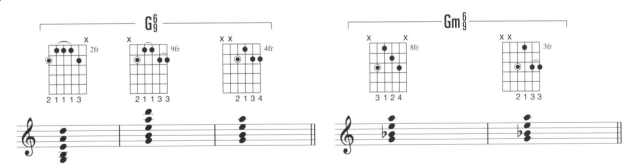

43

SEVENTH CHORDS

Seventh chords were discussed in depth in Chapter 6, so let's get right to the voicings. Fig. 9A features Cmaj7 chords. Major seventh chords (1–3–5–7) have a pretty sound and are useful for jazz, Latin, and pop ballads. Fig. 9B depicts Cm7 chords. Minor seventh chords (1–♭3–5–♭7) are a good alternative to minor chords, offering a bit more color. Also ubiquitous in jazz, they are quite common in funk, rock, and blues as well. Fig. 9C shows C7 chords. Dominant seventh chords (1–3–5–♭7) are prevalent in virtually every style of music. In Fig. 9D you'll find Cm7♭5 voicings. Minor seven flat-five chords (1–♭3–♭5–♭7) are most often associated with ii–V–i progressions in jazz, in which they function as the ii7♭5 in a minor key.

Figs. 9A–9B

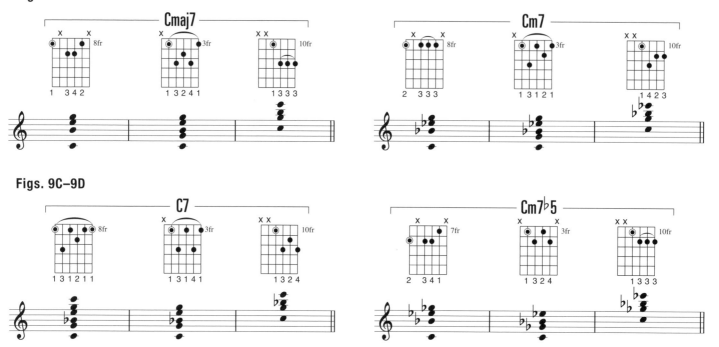

Figs. 9C–9D

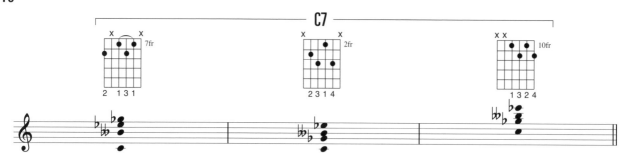

DIMINISHED SEVENTH, DOMINANT SEVENTH SUS4, AND MINOR(MAJ7) CHORDS

The diminished seventh chord is a diminished triad with an added double-flat (or diminished) 7th interval (1–♭3–♭5–♭♭7). It is often used as a non-diatonic (outside the key of the progression) passing chord when connecting two diatonic chords. A diminished seventh chord is a series of stacked minor 3rd intervals. Because of this, any note can be considered the root (Fig. 10).

Fig. 10

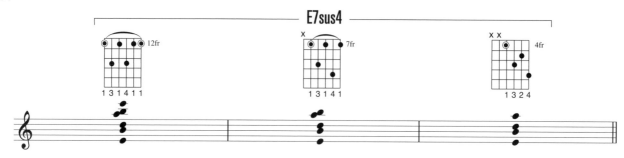

The dominant seventh sus4 chord is a dominant seventh chord with its 3rd removed and replaced with a 4th interval (1–4–5–♭7). These chords are often used in conjunction with their dominant seventh counterparts, as in E7sus4 releasing to E7 (Fig. 11).

Fig. 11

A minor(maj7) chord is a minor triad with an added major seventh interval (1–♭3–5–7). (See Fig. 12.) Usually used as a transition chord, you'll find it tucked between a minor triad and a minor seventh chord, as in Cm–Cm(maj7)–Cm7.

Fig. 12

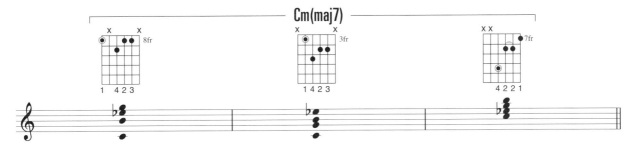

EXTENDED CHORDS

An extended chord is a seventh chord with an added extension of a 9th, 11th, 13th, or combination thereof. A major ninth chord is a major seventh chord with an added major ninth (1–3–5–7–9); a minor ninth chord is a minor seventh chord with an added major 9th (1–♭3–5–♭7–9); and a dominant ninth chord is a dominant seventh chord with an added major 9th degree (1–3–5–♭7–9). (See Fig. 13.) (Note: When the suffix "9" appears by itself, it represents a dominant ninth chord.)

Fig. 13

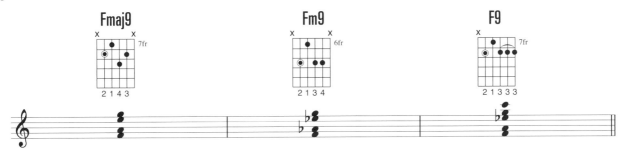

An eleventh chord is a seventh chord with the added extension of a perfect 11th. (An eleventh chord voicing doesn't need to include a 9th, but a 7th has to be present.) Minor eleventh chords (1–♭3–5–♭7–9–11) are often used in jazz fusion and progressive rock (Fig. 14A). Dominant eleventh chords (1–3–5–♭7–9–11) are prominent in styles such as jazz, funk, and R&B (Fig. 14B). (Note: When the suffix "11" appears by itself, it represents a dominant eleventh chord.) When the 11th is added to major seventh chord types, it is usually raised by a half step, so as not to clash with the major 3rd (see ♯11 chords, Fig. 19).

Figs. 14A–14B

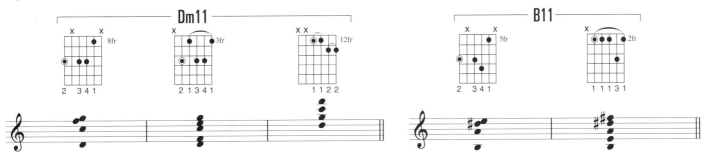

Thirteenth chords are much like ninth chords in that they are equally dispersed between major, minor, and dominant chord types. A major thirteenth chord is basically a major seventh chord with an added extension of a major 13th (1–3–5–7–13). Some major thirteenth voicings include the 9th, but generally not the 11th, as it clashes with the major 3rd of the chord (Fig. 15A). A minor thirteenth chord is a minor seventh chord with an added major 13th (1–♭3–5–♭7–13). Again, the 9th and 11th need not be present in the voicing to classify the chord as minor thirteenth (Fig. 15B). A dominant thirteenth chord is a dominant seventh chord with an added major 13th (1–3–5–♭7–13). Sometimes the 9th is included (Fig. 15C), and sometimes not (Fig. 15D). (Note: When the suffix "13" appears by itself, it represents a dominant thirteenth chord.

Figs. 15A–15B

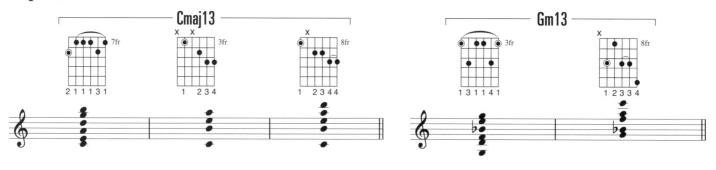

Figs. 15C–15D

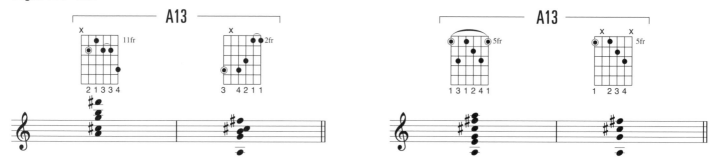

ALTERED CHORDS

When the 5th or 9th of a chord is lowered or raised by a half step, the result is an altered chord. The majority of altered chords are altered dominant chords. These are used for tension and usually, but not always, resolve down a 5th (or up a 4th) to their respective I or i chords. Fig. 16 shows voicings of a G7 chord with a ♯5th, ♭5th, ♭9th, and ♯9th. All would resolve nicely to a Cmaj7 or Cm7 chord. (Dominant seventh sharp nine chords often function as the I chord in funk and blues rock.)

Fig. 16

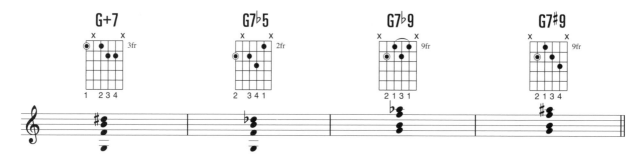

It's not uncommon to encounter dominant seventh chords with more than one alteration, as depicted in Fig. 17.

Fig. 17

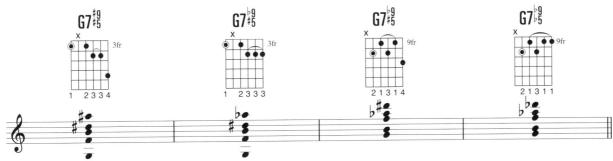

Fig. 18 offers some examples of extended chords with alterations. A sharp 11th is the enharmonic equivalent of a flat 5th. (Notes with the same pitch but different names are called enharmonic.)

Fig. 18

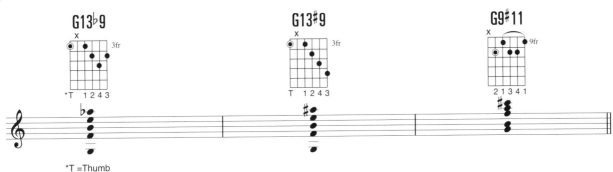

*T = Thumb

Major seventh sharp eleven (1–3–5–7–#11) and major seventh sharp five (1–3–#5–7) chords are common fixtures in jazz and jazz fusion (Fig. 19). (Minor chords don't generally receive alterations beyond the flat 5th.)

Fig. 19

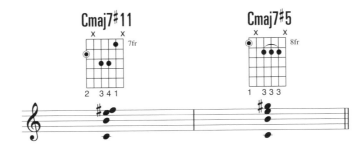

SLASH CHORDS

Slash chord notation is a modern method used to quickly describe specific chord voicings, without having to write them out on the staff. Slash chord symbols resemble mathematical fractions (1/2, 1/4, etc.) with chord and note names instead of numbers (A/B, G/B, etc.). The top letter (to the left of the slash) corresponds to the chord, while the bottom letter (to the right of the slash) indicates the bass note. Sometimes slash chord notation is used to indicate specific inversions of common chords, such as C/G (second inversion C chord) or G/B (first inversion G chord). However, slash chord symbols are also used to describe complex chords that are difficult to notate. Fig. 20 offers examples of slash chords, and the traditional names of the chords they imply.

Fig. 20

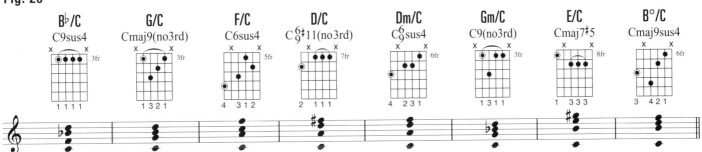

POLYCHORDS

A polychord is a combination of two chords (usually triads) that, when played together, create a more complex sound. Polychords are notated with a horizontal line, as opposed to the diagonal line used in slash chords. Polychords are popular among keyboard players, but they don't transfer easily to guitar. Fig. 21 offers a few "finger friendly" polychords to give you an idea of their intriguing sonic possibilities.

Fig. 21

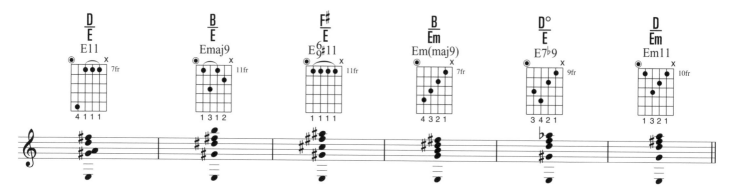

Quiz #8

(Answers are in the back of the book.)

1) What kind of triad provides the foundation of a maj9 chord? _____

2) What kind of triad provides the foundation of a m7♭5 chord? _____

3) What kind of 7th does a minor seventh chord contain? _____

4) Is E13 a major, minor, or dominant chord? _____

5) What is the 7th of a D9 chord? _____

6) Does a maj13 chord need to include the 11th? _____

7) What are the notes in an A°7 chord? ___ ___ ___ ___

8) What chord does B♭/C suggest? _____

9) Write the chord symbol for a first inversion G chord using slash chord notation. _____

10) True or False: Polychords are a cinch to play on the guitar. _____

CHAPTER 8: HARMONIZING THE MINOR SCALE

Just as the major scale is the source for major key chord progressions, the minor scale provides the harmony for minor keys. The minor scale can be harmonized using the exact same methods brought forth in Chapter 6.

MINOR SCALE TRIADS

To harmonize any minor scale, start by writing it out on the staff. (Let's use the A minor scale: Fig. 1A.) Next, stack a diatonic 3rd interval on top of each scale step (Fig. 1B). Finally, stack another diatonic 3rd interval on top of the second one (Fig. 1C). This last step results in the diatonic triads of the A minor scale.

Figs. 1A–1C

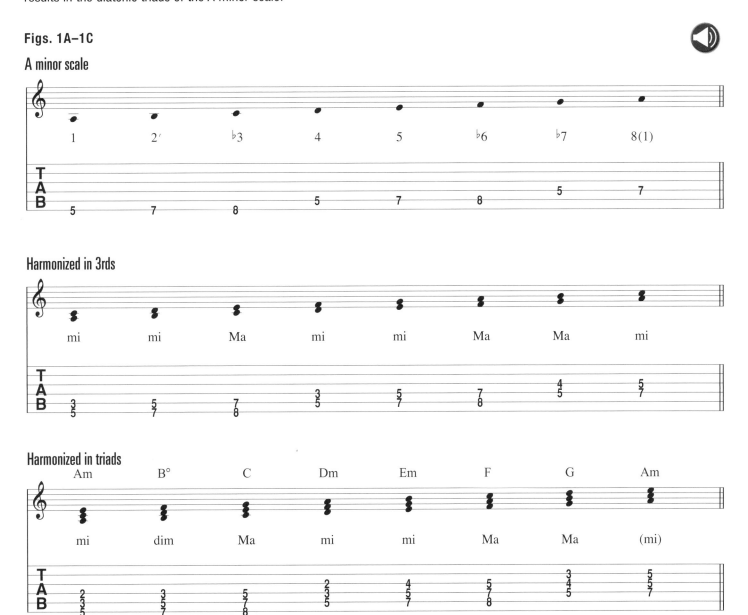

Fig. 2 shows the formula for harmonized triads of the minor scale: i–ii°–♭III–iv–v–♭VI–♭VII. Again, lowercase Roman numerals indicate a minor triad, uppercase numerals indicate major triads, and the small circle (°) after the ii chord represents diminished. Notice that the III, VI, and VII chords are flatted (♭III, ♭VI, ♭VII). This of course is due to their corresponding scale steps.

Fig. 2

i	ii°	♭III	iv	v	♭VI	♭VII
Am	B°	C	Dm	Em	F	G

In Chapter 3 we learned that every minor scale has a relative major scale that shares the same notes and the same key signature. This same "relative" principle applies to minor and major scale harmonies as well. For example, A minor is relative to C major, so they share the same triads. Though they are still in alphabetical order, the sequence starts on a different tonic chord: Am or C (Fig. 3).

Fig. 3

	i	ii°	♭III	iv	v	♭VI	♭VII		
A minor:	Am	B°	C	Dm	Em	F	G		

		I	ii	iii	IV	V	vi	vii°
C major:		C	Dm	Em	F	G	Am	B°

This does not mean that the two keys are the same, though. Am is the central chord in the key of A minor, and C is the central chord for C major. It's just that it can be helpful for memorization purposes to realize they contain the same chords. Once you become accustomed to minor keys, it will be easier to view them as separate entities, apart from major. Until then, here's a reference chart of the harmonized triads in minor keys (Fig. 4).

Fig. 4

Harmonized Minor Scales (Triads)

Key	I	ii°	♭III	iv	v	♭VI	♭VII
A minor	Am	B°	C	Dm	Em	F	G
E minor	Em	F#°	G	Am	Bm	C	D
B minor	Bm	C#°	D	Em	F#m	G	A
F# minor	F#m	G#°	A	Bm	C#m	D	E
C# minor	C#m	D#°	E	F#m	G#m	A	B
G# minor	G#m	A#°	B	C#m	D#m	E	F#
E♭ minor	E♭m	F°	G♭	A♭m	B♭m	C♭	D♭
B♭ minor	B♭m	C°	D♭	E♭m	Fm	G♭	A♭
F minor	Fm	G°	A♭	B♭m	Cm	D♭	E♭
C minor	Cm	D°	E♭	Fm	Gm	A♭	B♭
G minor	Gm	A°	B♭	Cm	Dm	E♭	F
D minor	Dm	E°	F	Gm	Am	B♭	C

MINOR SCALE SEVENTH CHORDS

Once you've harmonized the minor scale in triads, it's easy to harmonize it in seventh chords. Simply stack another diatonic 3rd on top of each of the triads (Fig. 5).

Fig. 5

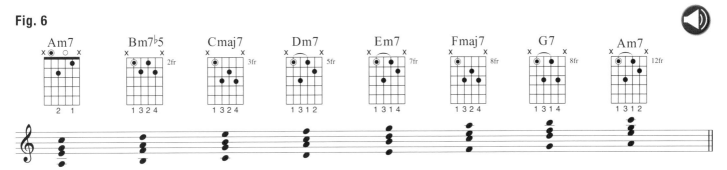

Again, the closed voicings in Fig. 5 require some pretty outrageous stretches. Fig. 6 demonstrates some more practical (open) voicings for these chords.

Fig. 6

Now we have the formula for the minor scale harmonized in seventh chords: i7–iim7♭5–♭IIImaj7–iv7–v7–♭VImaj7–♭VII7. Again, once you've memorized the formula, it's easy to harmonize the minor scale in any key. Fig. 7 offers a reference chart.

Fig. 7

Harmonized Minor Scales (Seventh Chords)

Key	i7	ii7♭5	♭IIImaj7	iv7	v7	♭VImaj7	♭VII7
A minor	Am7	Bm7♭5	Cmaj7	Dm7	Em7	Fmaj7	G7
E minor	Em7	F♯m7♭5	Gmaj7	Am7	Bm7	Cmaj7	D7
B minor	Bm7	C♯m7♭5	Dmaj7	Em7	F♯m7	Gmaj7	A7
F♯ minor	F♯m7	G♯m7♭5	Amaj7	Bm7	C♯m7	Dmaj7	E7
C♯ minor	C♯m7	D♯m7♭5	Emaj7	F♯m7	G♯m7	Amaj7	B7
G♯ minor	G♯m7	A♯m7♭5	Bmaj7	C♯m7	D♯m7	Emaj7	F♯7
E♭ minor	E♭m7	Fm7♭5	G♭maj7	A♭m7	B♭m7	C♭maj7	D♭7
B♭ minor	B♭m7	Cm7♭5	D♭maj7	E♭m7	Fm7	G♭maj7	A♭7
F minor	Fm7	Gm7♭5	A♭maj7	B♭m7	Cm7	D♭maj7	E♭7
C minor	Cm7	Dm7♭5	E♭maj7	Fm7	Gm7	A♭maj7	B♭7
G minor	Gm7	Am7♭5	B♭maj7	Cm7	Dm7	E♭maj7	F7
D minor	Dm7	Em7♭5	Fmaj7	Gm7	Am7	B♭maj7	C7

Quiz #9

This quiz covers material in this chapter and provides a review of Chapter 6 (Harmonizing the Major Scale). (Answers are in the back of the book.)

1) What are the iv and v chords (triads) in the key of E minor? _____ _____

2) What is the V chord (triad) of E major? _____

3) What is the ♭VI (seventh chord form) of D minor? _____

4) What is the vi (seventh chord form) of D major? _____

5) What are i–iv–v (seventh chords) in G minor? ___ ___ ___

6) What are I–IV–V (seventh chords) in G major? ___ ___ ___

7) What is the vii chord (triad) of A major? _____

8) What is the ♭VII chord (triad) of A minor? _____

9) What is the relative minor key of G major? _____

10) What is the relative major key of B minor? _____

11) The ♭III chord in the key of A minor is the _____ chord in the key of C major.

12) The vi chord in the key of C major is the _____ chord in the key of A minor.

Ear Training Drill #3

The following ear training drill involves short chord progressions in major and minor keys. All chords played are in root position. (Answers are in the back of the book.)

In Section A, the progression will be either I–IV–V–I (triad chords) in a major key, or i–iv–v–i in a minor key. Write your answers (major or minor) in the blanks provided.

Section A

1) _____   5) _____

2) _____   6) _____

3) _____   7) _____

4) _____

In Section B, the progression will be either I–vi–V–I (triad chords) in a major key, or i–♭VI–v–i in a minor key. Write your answers (major or minor) in the blanks provided.

Section B

8) _____   12) _____

9) _____   13) _____

10) _____   14) _____

11) _____

Section C is either Imaj7–IVmaj7–Imaj7 in a major key, or i7–iv7–i7 in a minor key. Write your answers (major or minor) in the blanks provided.

Section C

15) _____   19) _____

16) _____   20) _____

17) _____   21) _____

18) _____

CHAPTER 9: DETERMINING KEY CENTERS

Many guitarists learn to improvise over "changes" (chord progressions) by utilizing the key-center approach. This is the process of grouping as many chords as possible into a single major or minor key, thus allowing the use of one scale to create melodies for that group of chords.

Determining the key of a song or progression is not difficult when a key signature is involved. The problem is, many charts don't contain a key signature, and even when they do, some songs modulate to different keys without a change in the key signature. In these situations, you need to be able to tell what key a progression belongs to by means of the chords alone. Instinctive soloists can often find the key simply by listening. But it is also possible to determine the key by analyzing the relationship of the chords. Identifying the key that a group of chords belongs to is called *determining the key center.*

MAJOR KEY CENTERS

Determining the key center for a major progression is largely a process of elimination. For instance, the progression in Fig. 1 contains five different chords. Keeping in mind that there are two major seventh chords (Imaj7 and IVmaj7), three minor sevenths (ii7, iii7, and vi7), one dominant seventh (V7), and one minor seventh flat five chord (vii7♭5) in a single major key, list the possible keys under each chord. (Ex.: Fmaj7 could either be the I chord in F or the IV chord in C; Am7 could be the ii chord in G, the iii chord in F, or the vi chord in C.)

Fig. 1

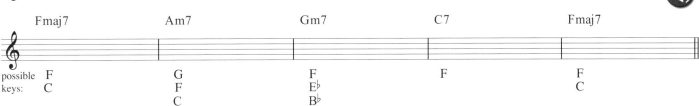

Now compare the candidates to find the one key to which all of the chords belong. The only possible answer is F. This means that the chord progression is in the key of F major, and that the F major scale is a suitable scale to use when creating melodies over this progression.

Now that we know the progression is in the key of F, let's write in the *function* for each chord (how the chord relates to the key center) using Roman numerals (Fig. 2).

Fig. 2

This discloses two important clues about the progression: 1) the presence of the V chord (C7); and 2) the fact that the progression begins and ends on the I chord (Fmaj7). The presence of a V chord is a dead giveaway for determining major key centers. Also, the first or last chord in a progression is often the I chord. Use these clues and the aforementioned steps to determine the key centers for the following progressions (Fig. 3), and then write the Roman numerals below each chord. Warning: Not all of the progressions contain V chords. (Answers are located on the next page after the last progression.)

Fig. 3

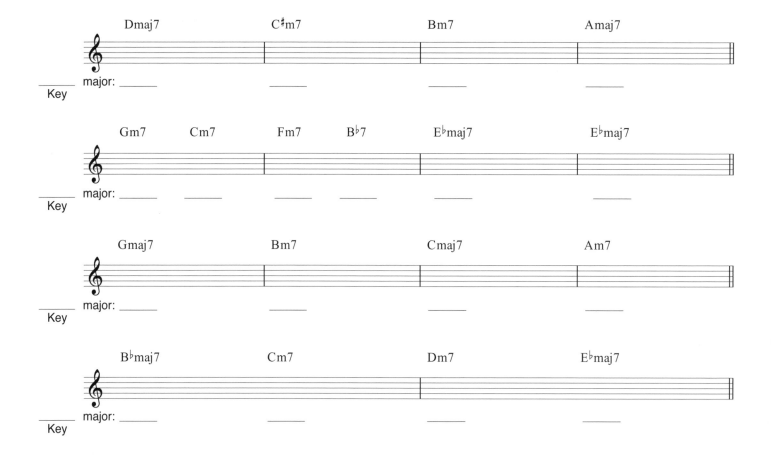

Answers:

C major: ii7–V7–IVmaj7–Imaj7

A major: IVmaj7–iii7–ii7–Imaj7

E♭ major: iii7–vi7–ii7–V7–Imaj7–Imaj7

G major: Imaj7–iii7–IVmaj7–ii7

B♭ major: Imaj7–ii7–iii7–IVmaj7

MINOR KEY CENTERS

Minor key centers can be determined using techniques similar to the ones we just covered: locating the central (tonic) chord, spotting "red flag" (giveaway) chords, and tenaciously following the process of elimination.

The following progression (Fig. 4) is in a minor key. Without looking at the answers (below the staff), write down the possible keys that each chord might belong to on a separate sheet of paper. (Remember: the minor seventh chords could be either the i, iv, or v; maj7 chords could be the ♭III or ♭VI; the Dom7 is the ♭VII, and a m7♭5 chord would be the ii.)

Fig. 4

Em7	Cmaj7	Am7	Bm7	Em7
possible keys: E minor	A minor	A minor	B minor	E minor
B minor	E minor	E minor	F♯ minor	B minor
A minor		D minor	E minor	A minor

When you're finished, check your results with the answers written below the staff. Then, using the process of elimination, figure out which minor key all of the chords belong to. If your analysis is correct, your answer will be the key of E minor (Fig. 5).

Fig. 5

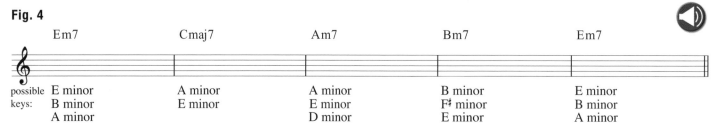

Em7	Cmaj7	Am7	Bm7	Em7
i7	♭VImaj7	iv7	v7	i7

In the "real world" of minor keys, things are sometimes more complicated. For instance, the v chord is often converted to a major triad or dominant seventh chord (Fig. 6), so as to contain the *leading tone*. The leading tone is the major 7th scale degree, which in turn leads upward by a half step to the tonic, creating a powerful sense of resolution. The major scale already contains the leading tone of course, but the 7th degree of the minor scale is a whole step below the tonic, making the pull to resolution much less dramatic.

Fig. 6

The V7 chord in minor keys can lead to confusion, because the ♭VII chord is also dominant in quality. But there is still a "dead giveaway" chord in minor keys: the m7♭5, which functions as the ii chord. Also, half-step root movement, from the ♭VI to the V (and vice versa) is a common occurrence in minor keys. With these clues in hand, go to work deciphering the following minor-key chord progressions (Fig. 7). (Answers are located after the last progression.)

Fig. 7

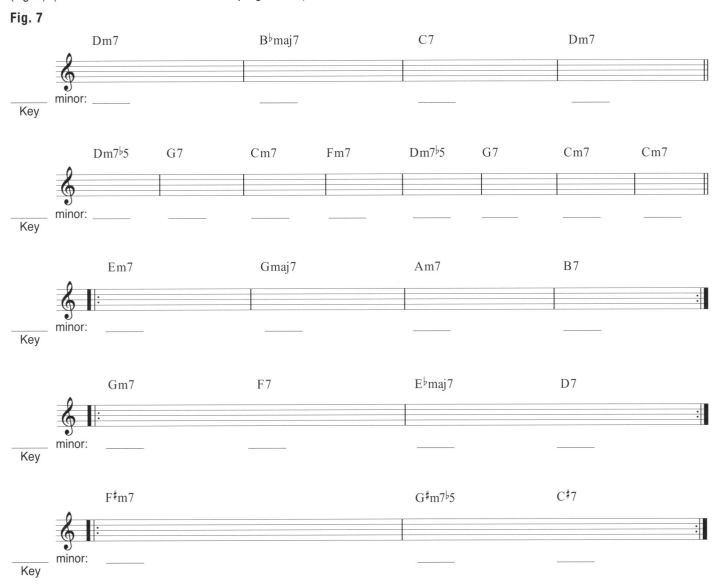

Answers:

D minor: i7–♭VImaj7–♭VII7–i7

C minor: ii7♭5–V7–i7–iv7–ii7♭5–V7–i7–i7

E minor: i7–♭IIImaj7–iv7–V7

G minor: i7–♭VII7–♭VImaj7–V7

F# minor: i7–ii7♭5–V7

TRIAD PROGRESSIONS

Triad progressions can be more difficult to analyze because the playing field is somewhat leveled. For instance, in major scale triad harmony, there are now three major chords (I, IV, and V), three minor chords (ii, iii, and vi), and one diminished chord (vii°). The same goes for minor keys, but in different categories: three minor triads: i–iv–v; three major triads: ♭III, ♭VI, and ♭VII; and one diminished: ii°. This means there is no dominant seventh "give-away" chord. With patience and practice, however, triad progressions won't be any more difficult to decipher than seventh chord progressions. Here are a few progressions to help you hone your chops (Fig. 8). (Answers are located after the last progression.)

Fig. 8

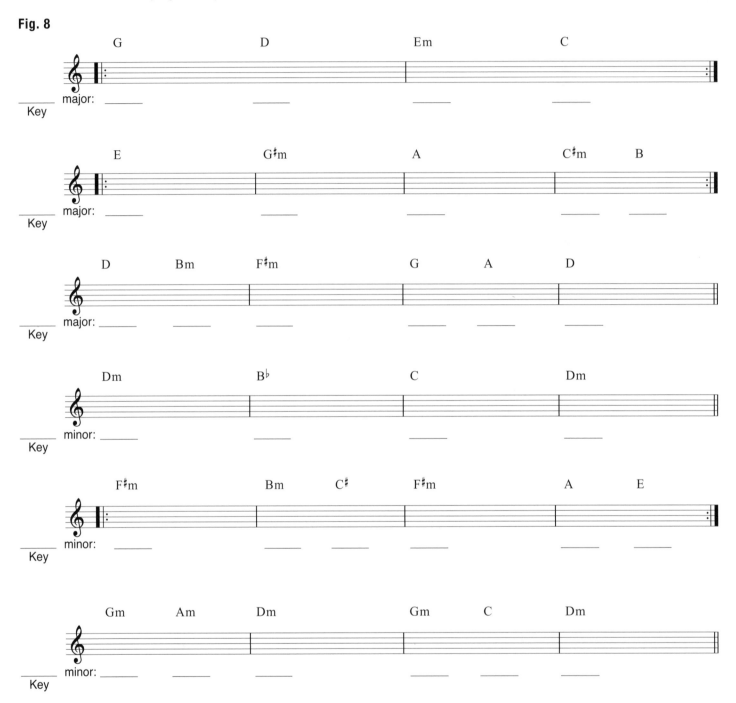

Answers:

G major: I–V–vi–IV

E major: I–iii–IV–vi–V

D major: I–vi–iii–IV–V–I

D minor: i–♭VI–♭VII–i

F♯ minor: i–iv–V–i–♭III–♭VII

D minor: iv–v–i–iv–♭VII–i

MODULATION

Some songs, especially jazz standards, move between two or more keys. Some even shift from major keys to minor keys, and vice versa. This transitioning of key centers is called *modulation*. Fig. 9 depicts a modulation from the key of C major to the key of B♭ major. This sudden change of keys is called *direct modulation*. Using the key-center approach, you would play the C major scale for the first two measures, and the B♭ major scale for measures 3–4.

Fig. 9

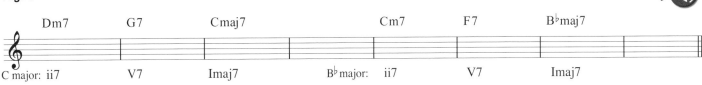

Fig. 10 moves from A minor to G major. Notice that the Am7 chord belongs to both keys: it's the i chord in A minor, and the ii chord in G major. This is an example of pivot chord modulation. Am7 is the *pivot chord,* or gateway chord, which provides a smooth transition from one key to the other. The key-center approach would be to play the A minor scale in the first half of the progression, and the G major scale in the second half. The pivot chord could receive either scale. The choice is up to the soloist.

Fig. 10

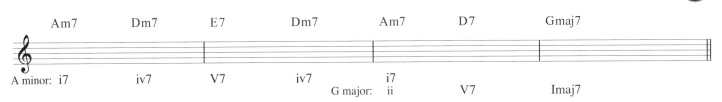

Here are six progressions that modulate from one key to another (Fig. 11). The first three are examples of direct modulation. The last three use a pivot chord to modulate to the new key. Fill in the correct keys and Roman numerals for each progression. (Answers are located on the next page after the last progression.)

Fig. 11

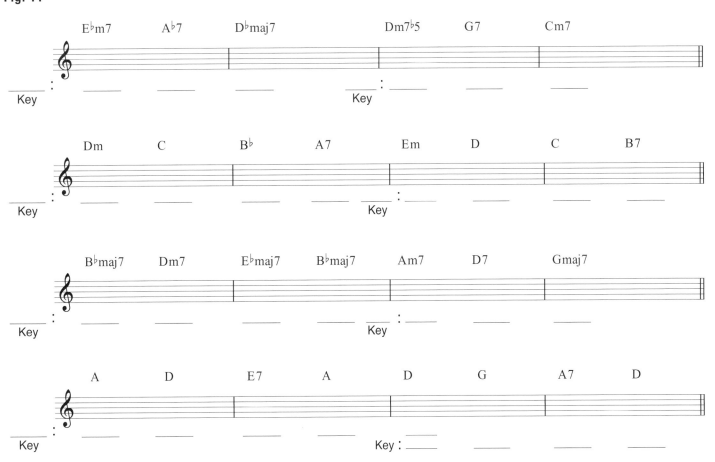

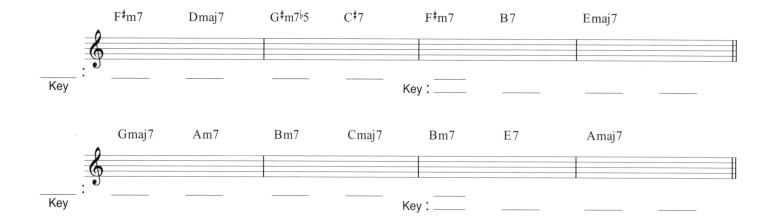

Answers:

D♭ major: ii7–V7–Imaj7, direct modulation to C minor: ii7♭5–V7–i7

D minor: i–♭VII–♭VI–V7, direct modulation to E minor: i–♭VII–♭VI–V7

B♭ major: Imaj7–iii7–IVmaj7–Imaj7, direct modulation to G major: ii7–V7–Imaj7

A major: I–IV–V7–I, pivot chord modulation to D major: I–IV–V7–I (D is the pivot chord: IV in A major, I in D major)

F♯ minor: i7–♭VImaj7–ii7♭5–V7, pivot chord modulation to E major: ii7–V7–Imaj7(F♯m7 is the pivot chord: i7 in F♯ minor, ii7 in E major)

G major: Imaj7–ii7–iii7–IVmaj7, pivot chord modulation to A major: ii7–V7–Imaj7(Bm7 is the pivot chord: iii7 in G major, ii7 in A major)

MODAL INTERCHANGE

Modal interchange is the temporary convergence of two parallel, major and minor key centers, in a single progression. Not to be confused with relative keys, which share the same notes and key signatures, *parallel* major and minor keys have different notes and harmonies, but share the same *tonic*. For example, C major is parallel to C minor; F minor is parallel to F major; and so on.

Fig. 12 offers an example of modal interchange. The majority of the progression is in the key of C major, but in the fourth measure a strange thing occurs. The quality of the IV chord (F) is converted to minor (Fm). When this occurs, we say the Fm chord is being temporarily "borrowed" from the parallel key of C minor.

Fig. 12

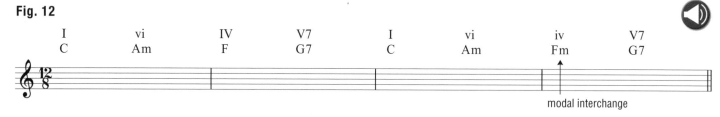

To understand modal interchange, we need to compare the differences and similarities between major and minor scale harmony. In Fig. 13A, the top row of chords represents the harmonized triads in the key of C major. Below them are the triads from the parallel key of C minor. The only similarities are that the roots of the I, ii, IV, and V chords are the same. Everything else is different: the chord qualities, and the root placement of the chords built off the 3rd, 6th, and 7th degrees. Fig. 13B compares the harmony of the two scales in seventh chord form.

Fig. 13A

Triads

	I	ii	iii	IV	V	vi	vii°
Key of C major:	C	Dm	Em	F	G	Am	B°
	i	ii°	♭III	iv	v	♭VI	♭VII
Key of C minor:	Cm	D°	E♭	Fm	Gm	A♭	B♭

Fig. 13B

Seventh Chords

	Imaj7	ii7	iii7	IVmaj7	V7	vi7	vii7♭5
Key of C major:	Cmaj7	Dm7	Em	Fmaj7	G7	Am7	Bm7♭5

	i7	ii7♭5	♭IIImaj7	iv7	v7	♭VImaj7	♭VII7
Key of C minor:	Cm7	Dm7♭5	E♭maj7	Fm7	Gm7	A♭maj7	B♭7

Now, take a look at the progression in Fig. 14. It begins with the I, iii, and IV of C major, but the fourth measure borrows the iv chord from the parallel key of C minor. We then slip back into C major with the iii and vi chords, borrow the ii chord from C minor, and go out with a V–I in C major again. The Fm7 and Dm7♭5 chords are the modal interchange chords. What do you do if you want to solo over the progression? The answer is quite simple: For the C major harmony part of the progression, play the C major scale. For the modal interchange chords, play the scale from which they are derived (or "borrowed")—in this case, the C minor scale.

Fig. 14

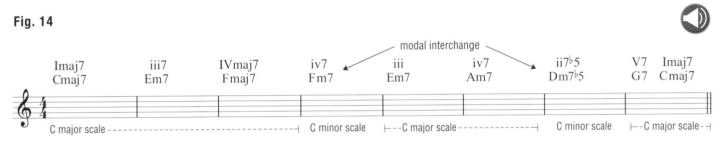

Fig. 15 features modal interchange in a C minor progression. The C minor scale would be the best source for melodies over the i, v, and ♭III chords, and the C major scale could be used over the modal interchange chord, C.

Fig. 15

The following progressions (Fig. 16) all include modal interchange. Write in the key, the chord functions, and indicate the modal interchange chord(s). (Answers are located on the next page after the last progression.)

Fig. 16

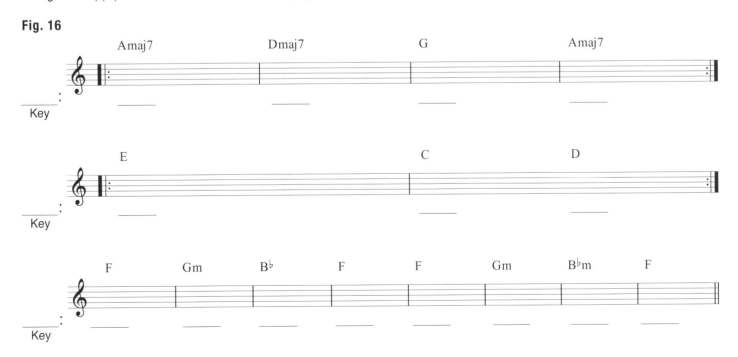

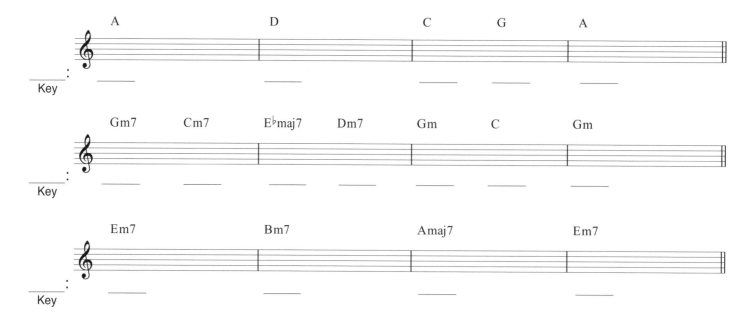

Answers:

A major: Imaj7–IVmaj7–♭VII–Imaj7, G is the modal interchange chord

E major: I–♭VI–♭VII, C and D are the modal interchange chords

F major: I–ii–IV–I–I–ii–iv–I, B♭m is the modal interchange chord

A major: I–IV–♭III–♭VII–I, C and G are the modal interchange chords

G minor: i7–iv7–♭VImaj7–v7–i–IV–i, C is the modal interchange chord

E minor: i7–v7–IVmaj7–i7, Amaj7 is the modal interchange chord

Ear Training Drill #4

Major or Minor Progressions

The following progressions are in a single major or minor key. Circle the correct answer. Some contain triad chords, some contain seventh chords. In all cases, the tonic note is played before each progression. (Answers are in the back of the book.)

1)   Major or minor

2)   Major or minor

3)   Major or minor

4)   Major or minor

5)   Major or minor

6)   Major or minor

7)   Major or minor

8)   Major or minor

Modal Interchange

The following major key progressions may or not include modal interchange. Circle "yes" if they do, and "no" if they don't. (Answers are in the back of the book.)

1)   Yes or no

2)   Yes or no

3)   Yes or no

4)   Yes or no

5)   Yes or no

CHAPTER 10: BLUES HARMONY AND PENTATONIC SCALES

So far we have been discussing harmony in traditional music theory terms. Blues (an American art form which blends elements of African and European music), challenges many of these rules.

THE 12-BAR BLUES PROGRESSION

Traditional blues is based on a I–IV–V chord system, that is, the I, IV, and V chords of the major scale. However, blues music emphasizes dominant seventh chords—not only applying them to the V chord, but to the I and IV as well. This tosses many of the rules of diatonic harmony right out the window. However, blues harmony is so ingrained in our pop music psyche that our ears accept it as normal.

The basic template for blues music is the "12-bar blues progression" (Fig. 1), a 12-bar system that is usually continually cycled throughout an entire song. The progression is split into three sections of four measures each. In these three sections, the I, IV, and V chords have their designated slots. The first section introduces the I chord, which establishes the key. The middle section moves to the IV chord, then back to the I. The third section is the most active. It begins with all three chords in descending succession (V–IV–I), then ends on what is called a *turnaround*. The turnaround section in blues appears in the last two measures, and usually comprises a I–♭VI–V cadence. It is called the turnaround because it "turns" the progression around to start at the beginning again.

Fig. 1

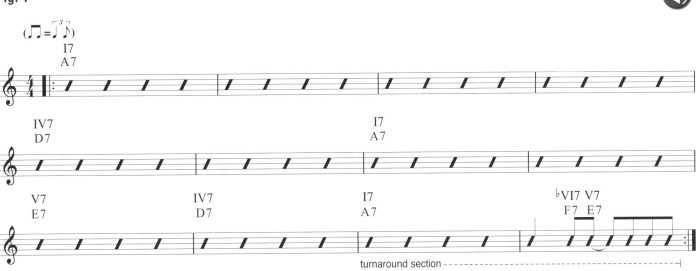

A common occurrence in 12-bar blues is the *quick change*. This is when the four measures of the I chord in the beginning are interrupted by one measure (measure 2) of the IV chord (Fig. 2). Other than this, the progression remains the same.

Fig. 2

12-bar blues progressions are repeated many times before the song reaches its conclusion. Fig. 3 features a standard ending for a 12-bar blues. This replaces the turnaround measures.

Fig. 3

Blues music is usually, but not always, played in a shuffle, or eighth-note shuffle rhythm. Tying together the first two notes of an eighth-note triplet grouping, leaving the third note unaltered, creates the eighth-note shuffle feel (Fig. 4).

Fig. 4

Notated at the beginning of a piece of music as:

OTHER BLUES PROGRESSIONS

Another popular I–IV–V blues progression is the *8-bar blues.* 8-bar blues progressions come in a variety of I–IV–V patterns. Figs. 5A & 5B offer typical examples of 8-bar blues.

Fig. 5A

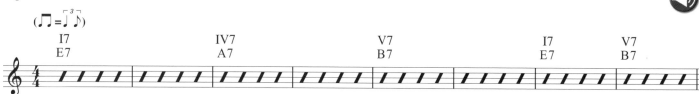

Fig. 5B

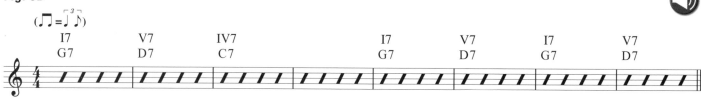

Still another standard blues progression is the *16-bar blues.* Fig. 6 offers an example in the key of C.

Fig. 6

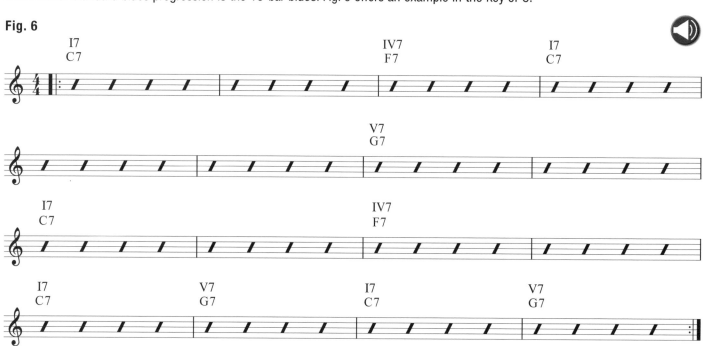

Blues music occasionally draws from diatonic harmony, most often in minor keys. A *minor blues* typically follows the 12-bar format, but utilizes minor scale changes (i–iv–v), rather than dominant seventh chords. Minor seventh voicings are often used, and it's not uncommon to include ♭VImaj7, as well as altered V7 chords (Fig. 7).

Fig. 7

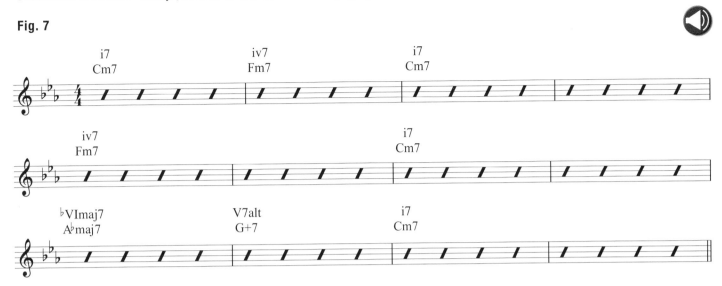

MINOR PENTATONIC AND BLUES SCALE

Blues melodies and solos rely heavily on the *minor pentatonic scale*. The minor pentatonic scale is a five-note scale (the word pentatonic has Greek origins: *penta* meaning five, and *tonos* meaning tone) derived from the natural minor scale. (Note: The term *natural minor* scale simply refers to the minor scale, or relative minor scale of the major scale. It is used mainly when being compared to other minor-scale types, which will be discussed later.) Specifically, it is made up of the root, ♭3rd, 4th, 5th, and ♭7th scale degrees of the minor scale (minor pentatonic formula: 1–♭3–4–5–♭7). This essentially omits the "awkward" half-step intervals, which are normally located between the 2nd and the ♭3rd, and the 5th and ♭6th scale tones. Fig. 8 depicts this conversion process applied to the A minor scale.

Fig. 8

Removing the half-step intervals creates minor 3rd scale gaps between the root and ♭3rd, and the 5th and ♭7th. This actually transfers to finger-friendly, two-note-per-string patterns on the fretboard—small wonder it is so popular among guitarists of all styles, from rock to jazz. Fig. 9 shows six patterns of the A minor pentatonic scale. The sixth pattern is actually the same as the open-position pattern, just an octave up.

Fig. 9

A minor pentatonic

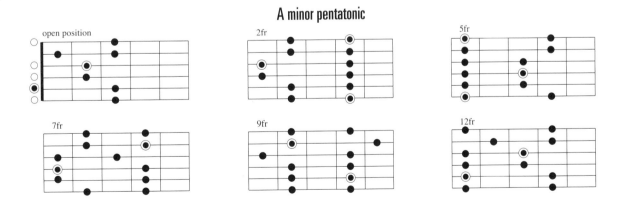

The minor pentatonic scale acts as a "one scale serves all" in I–IV–V blues progressions. When used to its full potential, its unique properties provide a wealth of interesting chord tone possibilities. Fig. 10 shows the chord-coloring potential of the A minor pentatonic scale when used in an A blues setting. The #9th (C against the A7 chord, and G against the E7 chord), and the #5th are referred to as *blue notes,* or tension notes that technically clash with the harmony. (Note: The minor pentatonic scale is also an excellent scale choice for minor-key applications.)

Fig. 10

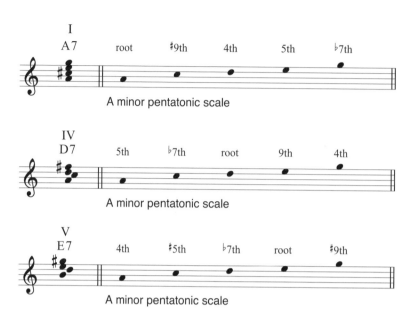

Another scale, so widespread in blues music that it gets its name from the genre itself, is the blues scale. The blues scale is a six-note scale comprised of the notes of the minor pentatonic scale, but with an added ♭5th degree (blues scale formula: 1–♭3–4–♭5–5–♭7). The ♭5th provides a unique *chromatic passage* (half-step sequence) from the 4th to the 5th scale degrees. Fig. 11 shows the A blues scale on the staff, along with two popular scale patterns.

Fig. 11

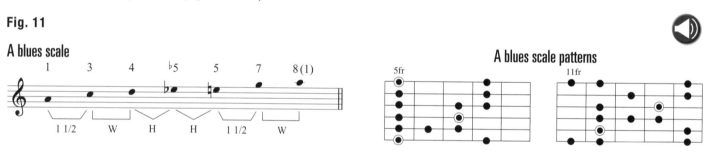

In an A blues setting, the ♭5th (E♭) of the A blues scale provides a ♭5th against the I chord (A7), a ♭9th against the IV chord (D7), and a major 7th against the V chord (E7). While the blue note (the ♭5th) is usually not leaned on too much, it provides the characteristic "tough" sound popular in blues music when used in passing.

MAJOR PENTATONIC SCALE

Still another popular scale used in blues, and virtually all other styles as well, is the *major pentatonic scale.* The major pentatonic scale is a five-note scale derived from the major scale. Specifically, it consists of the root, 2nd, 3rd, 5th, and 6th scale degrees of the major scale (major pentatonic formula: 1–2–3–5–6). In similar fashion to the minor pentatonic scale, this eliminates the half-step intervals between certain scale steps. In the major scale, these are between the 3rd and the 4th, and the 7th and the octave. Fig. 12A depicts the major-pentatonic conversion process applied to the C major scale, and Fig. 12B shows C major pentatonic scale patterns.

Fig. 12A

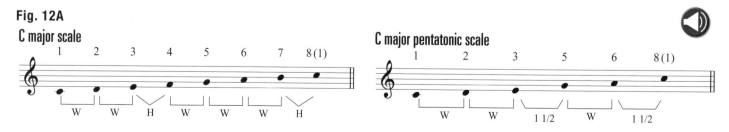

Fig. 12B

C major pentatonic

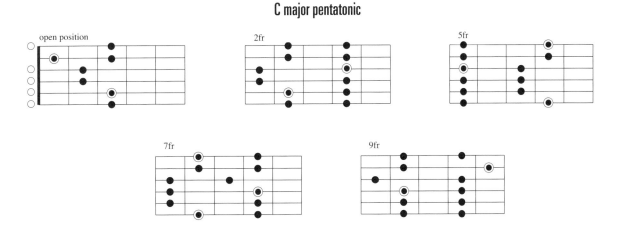

Notice that these patterns are similar to the A minor pentatonic scale patterns from Fig. 9. As a matter of fact they are exactly the same! The only exception is that the roots are different. Just as the C major scale is relative to the A minor scale, the C major pentatonic scale is relative to the A minor pentatonic scale, and vice versa. ("Relativity" concepts are discussed in depth in Chapter 11, "Modes.")

In some styles, especially rock and country, the major pentatonic scale is used as a stripped-down version of the major scale. In blues it is used selectively to service the I–IV–V dominant blues changes. Fig. 13 gives a rundown of the chord-tone possibilities within the C major pentatonic scale when applied to the I–IV–V chords in a C blues progression.

Fig. 13

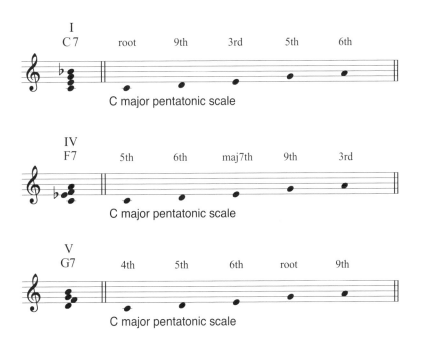

As you can see, with the exception of the major 7th rub against the IV chord (F7), most of the note selections are safe, sweet, inside choices: (roots, 3rds, 5ths, 9ths, 6ths).

PARALLEL PENTATONIC SCALES

In blues and blues-based music (such as blues rock and many forms of jazz), it's common practice to mix parallel major and minor pentatonic scales. Not to be confused with "relative scales" (two scales that share the same notes), *parallel scales* are scales that share the same tonic, or root. For instance, as we know, the A minor pentatonic and C major pentatonic scale are "relative." However, the A minor pentatonic scale is "parallel" to the A major pentatonic scale—two entirely different scales, but they share the same root. Fig. 14 shows what happens when you combine the A minor pentatonic with the A major pentatonic scale.

Fig. 14

A minor pentatonic

A major pentatonic

A minor pentatonic and A major pentatonic scales combined

Two of the notes overlap (root and 5th), but the end result is an eight-note scale that exhibits both major and minor (major 3rd and minor 3rd) properties. Usually reserved for the I chord in blues, it provides a cornucopia of chord tones. Fig. 15 shows overlapping A minor and A major pentatonic scales in pattern form.

Fig. 15

A major/minor pentatonic pattern

Quiz #10

(Answers are in the back of the book.)

1) What is the quick-change chord in 12-bar blues? _____

2) Where does it occur? _____

3) Where are the turnaround bars in a 12-bar blues? _____

4) How many notes are there in the minor pentatonic scale? _____

5) How many half-step intervals does it contain? _____

6) How many notes are there in the blues scale? _____

7) The ♭5th of the blues scale creates a ♭9th alteration for which chord: the I, the IV, or the V? _____

8) What is the formula for the major pentatonic scale? _____

9) What is the most common chord quality in blues? _____

10) The A minor pentatonic scale is *relative* to the _____ pentatonic scale.

11) The A minor pentatonic scale is *parallel* to the _____ pentatonic scale.

Ear Training Drill #5

In each example you will hear a scale played in two octaves. Decide if it is minor pentatonic, major pentatonic, or the blues scale. All examples start on the root of the scale. Write your answers in the blanks provided. (Answers are in the back of the book.)

1) _____   5) _____   9) _____

2) _____   6) _____   10) _____

3) _____   7) _____   11) _____

4) _____   8) _____   12) _____

CHAPTER 11:
MODES AND MODAL HARMONY

This chapter is a study of the seven modes of the major scale.

WHAT ARE MODES?

Modes are simply scales, or more precisely, "scales within scales." Every diatonic scale contains its own set of modes, but the modes of the major scale are by far the most common, and they will be the focus of this chapter.

Modes are created by shifting the tonal center away from the root—or tonic—of a scale, to another note of that same scale, thereby creating a new tonality. We've seen how this works with the relative minor scale (this is actually a mode), which is constructed from the sixth note of the major scale (Chapter 3). Let's review the process using a different note of the major scale.

When you play the C major scale from its root (C) to the octave, it has the familiar "do-re-mi-fa-sol-la-ti-do" major scale sound. This, of course, is due to the order of intervals, or intervallic formula: whole–whole–half–whole–whole–whole–half (Fig. 1).

Fig. 1

C major scale (root to root)

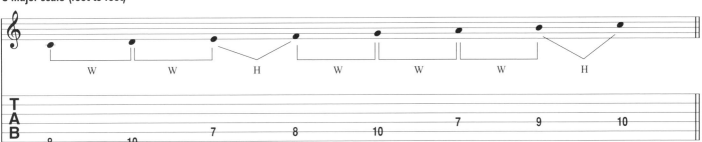

Now, if you play the C major scale again, but this time start from the second note (D) and play up to its octave (D), you will be playing the second "mode" of the C major scale (Fig. 2). Notice that it doesn't sound like C major anymore, even though you're playing the same notes. There is a simple explanation for this "phenomenon": you've shifted the order of intervals by starting on the second note of the scale. Now the intervallic formula reads: whole–half–whole–whole–whole–half–whole. Thus, "a scale within a scale."

Fig. 2

C major scale (D to D)

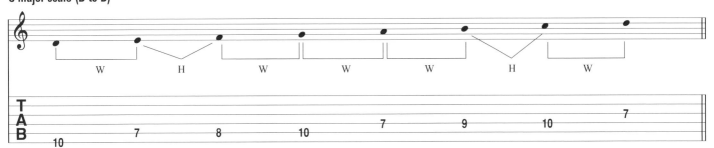

This process can be applied to the other notes of the C major scale as well. And since the C major scale has seven notes (C–D–E–F–G–A–B), it contains seven modes (Fig. 3). (Note: All major scales, no matter what key, have the same intervallic formula. Therefore, the process for constructing the seven modes of every major scale is exactly the same as illustrated in the key of C.)

Fig. 3

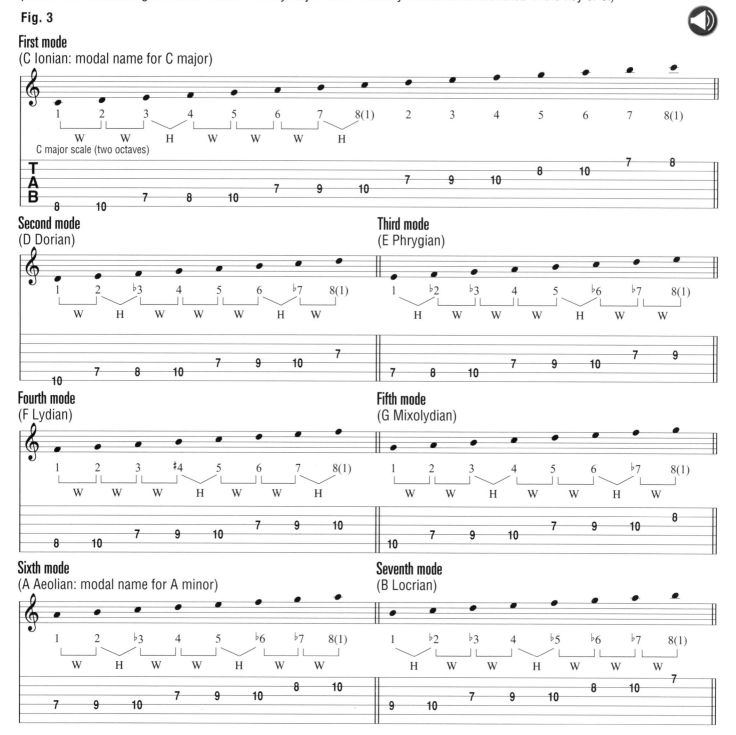

The names of the modes of the major scale have Greek origins. You'll want to memorize the names, the order, and their basic quality (major, minor, dominant, or diminished) as soon as possible.

	Mode	Pronunciation	Quality
1	**Ionian**	eye-own-ee-un	major
2	**Dorian**	door-ee-un	minor
3	**Phrygian**	fridge-ee-un	minor
4	**Lydian**	lid-ee-un	major
5	**Mixolydian**	mix-oh-lid-ee-un	dominant
6	**Aeolian**	ay-oh-lee-un	minor
7	**Locrian**	low-kree-un	diminished

The Parent Scale

The *parent scale* is the major scale from which a specific mode is derived. For example, C major is the parent scale of D Dorian. It is also the parent scale of G Mixolydian, F Lydian, and so on. The ability to recognize the parent scale is important for understanding modal concepts. Here is a three-step, fill-in-the-blanks process that will help you name the parent scale of any mode.

To find the parent scale of <u>A Mixolydian</u>:

Step 1) <u>Mixolydian</u> is the <u>fifth</u> mode.

Step 2) <u>A</u> is the <u>fifth</u> scale step of <u>D</u> major.

Step 3) <u>D</u> major is the parent scale of <u>A</u> <u>Mixolydian</u>.

Spend some time drilling yourself to find the parent scales to all of the modes, in as many keys as possible. Your knowledge of major scales and their key signatures will determine how rapidly you will find the answers. Here's a blank form you can work with:

To find the parent scale of ___ _____ :

Step 1) _____ is the _____ mode.

Step 2) ____ is the _____ scale step of ____ major.

Step 3) ____ major is the parent scale of ___ _____.

HOW MODES ARE USED

There are three main categorizations for how modes are used:

- As melodic devices for soloing over diatonic chord progressions in major and minor keys.
- As melodic devices for soloing over "modal" progressions.
- As a source for creating "altered" scales.

Modes in Major and Minor Scale Progressions

To understand how modes are used in diatonic chord progressions, it's necessary to have a working knowledge of major scale harmony. This was covered in Chapter 6, but let's do a quick review.

The notes of the major scale can be harmonized (stacked in 3rd intervals) to build diatonic triads and seventh chords from each scale degree. Here they are in the key of C (Fig. 4).

Fig. 4

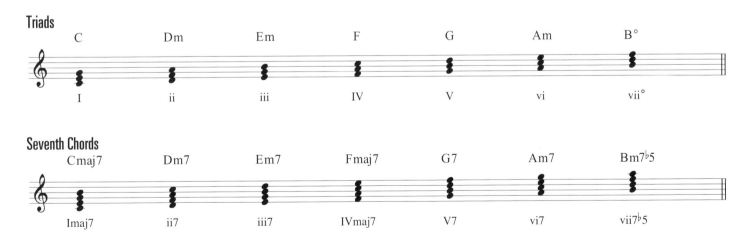

These chords constitute the harmonic palette for the key of C major—the range of possible harmonies you'll find in a diatonic progression. Each chord has a *quality* (major, minor, etc.) and a function (I, ii, iii, etc.) determined by its position within the scale. (Although the triads omit the seventh, the basic chord qualities and functions remain the same.) This results in a chord formula that applies to all major keys: Imaj7–ii7–iii7–IVmaj7–V7–vi7–vii7♭5. In Fig. 5 you'll find voicings of the seventh chords from C major. Play them (in order) up and down the neck, and you will hear the underlying sound of the major scale.

Fig. 5

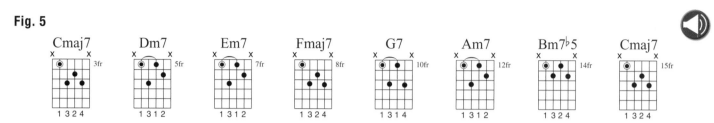

Just as there is a designated chord for each scale step, there is a corresponding mode for each chord. For example, over the ii7 chord in a C major progression, the ear wants to "hear" the corresponding mode—D Dorian—because it's the diatonic choice (Dm7 is the ii chord in C, and D Dorian is the second mode of C). Likewise, if the V7 (G7) chord comes along, the fifth mode (G Mixolydian) is the "proper" choice. Here's a straightforward, "hands-on" demonstration of how this concept works (Fig. 6). Have a friend play the chords while you play the exercise.

Fig. 6

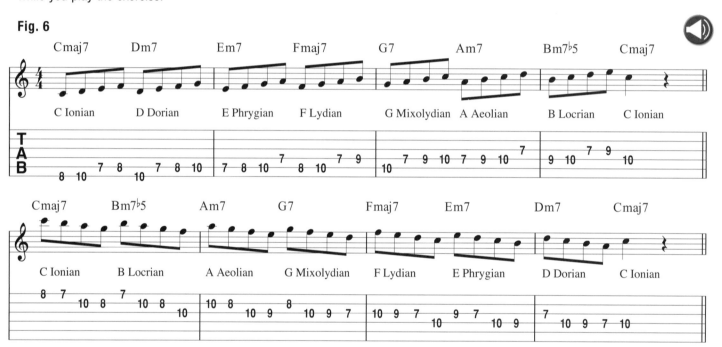

Every note of each mode is represented in this exercise. Keep in mind that in reality, this "modal" approach works best when a chord lasts long enough (one or more measures) for a melody to be fully developed.

Modes and Modal Progressions

We've witnessed how the major scale can be harmonized to create chords built from each scale degree. The same process can be applied to the modes to create *modal harmony*. When the chords from a specific mode are used to create a chord progression, it is called a *modal progression*. For example, if you were to harmonize D Dorian in seventh chords, the result would be: Dm7–Em7–Fmaj7–G7–Am7–Bm7♭5–Cmaj7 (Fig. 7).

Fig. 7

Harmonizing D Dorian

Dm7	Em7	Fmaj7	G7	Am7	Bm7♭5	Cmaj7	Dm7
i7	ii7	♭IIImaj7	IV7	v7	vi7♭5	♭VIImaj7	i7

Of course, these chords belong to C major—the parent scale of D Dorian—but now Dm7 is the tonic, or i chord, and each chord now serves a different function. If you were to build a progression around the Dm7 chord (i chord) using some or all of the other chords in the harmonized mode, you would be creating a modal progression—in this case, a D Dorian progression. D Dorian is now the key center, so the Dorian mode is the ideal choice for soloing (Fig. 8).

Fig. 8

Modes as "Altered" Scales

Theoretically, there are specific modes that the ear "wants" or "expects" to hear in a diatonic progression. But sometimes the element of surprise is desired while improvising, and it often surfaces in the form of dissonance, or tension. Superimposing modes and mixing-and-matching *parallel modes* (different modes that share the same root) can be handy improvisational tools for achieving this type of effect. For example, G Phrygian might be used where G Aeolian is the more likely candidate; A Lydian could be substituted for A Ionian; E Mixolydian and E Dorian might be juggled back and forth over an E7 chord for a delightfully bluesy outcome; etc.

In order for this modal style of playing to work, you need to follow some type of system, or the results will be chaotic. Grouping the modes into specific categories for comparison purposes is extremely helpful for this (and all other modal applications as well, for that matter). The chart below breaks the modes into two basic categories (major and minor) and then compares these to the properties of the major scale and minor scale.

Major Modes

- Ionian: major scale
- Lydian: major scale with a $\sharp$4
- Mixolydian: major scale with a $\flat$7th

Minor Modes

- Aeolian: minor scale
- Dorian: minor scale with a natural 6th
- Phrygian: minor scale with a $\flat$2nd
- Locrian: minor scale with a $\flat$5th and $\flat$2nd

THE MODES

Ionian

Formula:	1–2–3–4–5–6–7
Construction:	W–W–H–W–W–W–H
Category:	Major
Differentiating scale degree:	7th (Note: The "differentiating scale degree" is the note that sets this mode apart from other modes in the same category.)
For chord types:	major, 6, 6/9, maj7, maj9, maj13, add9
Harmony:	Imaj7–ii7–iii7–IVmaj7–V7–vi7–vii7$\flat$5
Common Progressions:	I–IV–I; ii–V–I; I–vi–IV–V; I–iii–IV–I; I–IV; I–V–I

Ionian outlines the basic structure of a major seventh chord (root, 3rd, 5th, 7th) and these extensions: 9th, 11th, and 13th.

Patterns for Ionian
(Roots are circled; notes in parentheses are the 7th degrees.)

Fig. 9

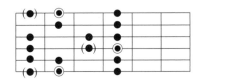
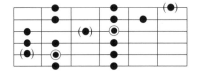
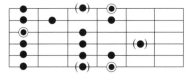

Ionian is the modal name for the major scale. It corresponds to the I chord in major keys, but it also aligns with the ♭III chord in minor key progressions. For example, in an E minor progression, Gmaj7 is the ♭III chord. If that chord comes along, G Ionian is the ideal mode to play because it is the "diatonic" mode in that situation (Fig. 10).

Fig. 10

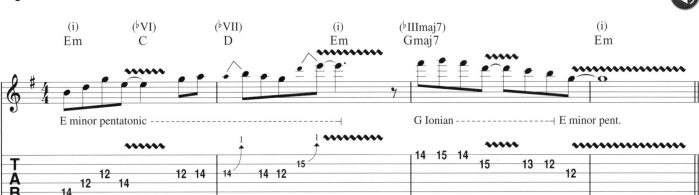

Dorian

Formula:	1–2–♭3–4–5–6–♭7
Construction:	W–H–W–W–W–H–W
Category:	Minor
Differentiating scale degree:	6th
For chord types:	minor, m6, m6/9, m7, m9, m13, m(add9)
Harmony:	i7–ii7–♭IIImaj7–IV7–v7–vi7♭5–♭VIImaj7
Common Progressions:	i–IV; i–ii; i–♭III–IV; i–v–IV–i; i–ii–♭III–ii

Dorian outlines the basic structure of a minor seventh chord (root, ♭3rd, 5th, ♭7th) and these extensions: 9th, 11th, and 13th.

Patterns for Dorian
(Roots are circled; notes in parentheses are the 6th degrees.)

Fig. 11

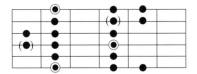
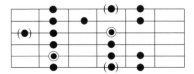
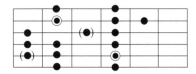

Dorian is the second mode of the major scale. It corresponds to the ii chord in major keys and the iv chord in minor key progressions. It has the same structure as the natural minor scale (Aeolian), except that it has a "raised" or natural 6th degree. This makes the scale sound lighter, softer, and a bit more mysterious than the "heavier," more dramatic Aeolian mode.

Dorian can be heard extensively in jazz, blues, and rock music, and is featured prominently in the blues-rock solos of guitarists such as Jimi Hendrix, Carlos Santana, Jimmy Page, and Robby Krieger. Fig. 12 offers an example of the A Dorian mode in a classic Latin-rock, i7–IV7 progression.

Fig. 12

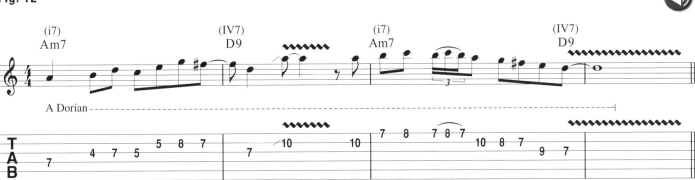

Phrygian

Formula:	1–♭2–♭3–4–5–♭6–♭7
Construction:	H–W–W–W–H–W–W
Category:	Minor
Differentiating scale degree:	♭2nd
For chord types:	m(♭9), m7(♭9), m(♭9, ♭6)
Harmony:	i7–♭IImaj7–♭III7–iv7–v7♭5–♭VImaj7–♭vii7
Common Progressions:	i–♭II; i–♭III–♭II; i–♭vii; i–♭II–i–♭vii

Phrygian outlines the basic structure of a minor seventh chord (root, ♭3rd, 5th, ♭7th) and these extensions: ♭9th, 11th, and ♭13th.

Patterns for Phrygian

(Roots are circled; notes in parentheses are the ♭2nd degrees.)

Fig. 13

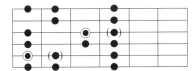  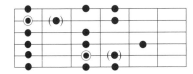

Phrygian is the third mode of the major scale. It corresponds to the iii chord in major keys and the v chord in minor key progressions. In iii chord applications it almost goes by unnoticed, but over the v chord in minor keys, and when isolated in a Phrygian progression, it has a very exotic sound. This is due mainly to the ♭2nd degree.

Phrygian makes its home in the adventurous progressions of jazz/fusion, but it also can be found in the rock world from vintage psychedelic bands like Jefferson Airplane and Quicksilver Messenger Service, to hardcore metal bands like Metallica and Megadeth. Fig. 14 offers an example of D Phrygian employed over a jazz-fusion style, Phrygian progression.

Fig. 14

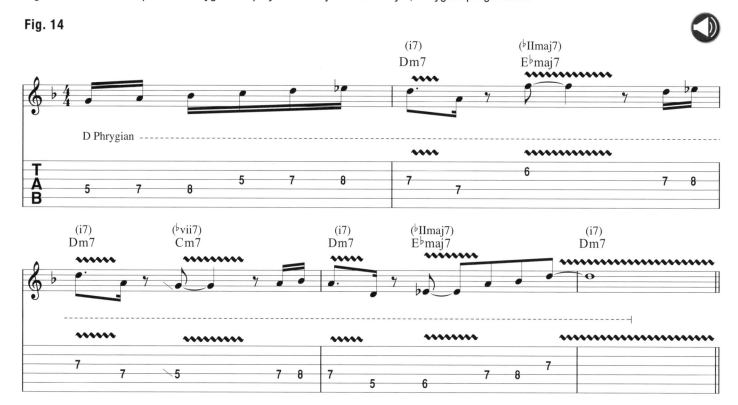

Lydian

Formula:	1–2–3–#4–5–6–7
Construction:	W–W–W–H–W–W–H
Category:	major
Differentiating scale degree:	#4th
For chord types:	major(#11); 6#11; 6/9#11; maj7#11; maj13#11
Harmony:	Imaj7–II7–iii7–#iv7♭5–Vmaj7–vi7–vii7
Common Progressions:	I–II; I–II–vii; I–vii; I–iii–vii

Lydian outlines the basic structure of a major seventh chord (root, 3rd, 5th, 7th) and these extensions: 9th, #11th, and 13th.

Patterns for Lydian

(Roots are circled; notes in parentheses are the #4th degrees.)

Fig. 15

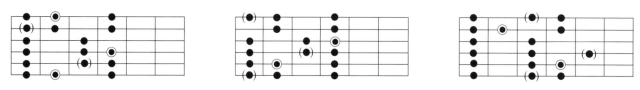

Lydian is the fourth mode of the major scale. It corresponds to the IV chord in major keys and the ♭VI chord in minor key progressions. Of all the modes, it is the closest in structure to that of the major scale (Ionian). The only difference is its #4th degree—seemingly a small difference, but it's significant. Whereas Ionian is consonant and familiar, Lydian has a "dreamy" and anticipatory nature. Often used in movie scores, Lydian is also a favorite choice among singer/songwriters like Stevie Nicks and Joni Mitchell. In the hands of guitarists like Joe Satriani and Steve Vai, Lydian can bring tears to your eyes. Fig. 16 offers a soul-stirring example of G Lydian over a classic, I–II Lydian progression.

Fig. 16

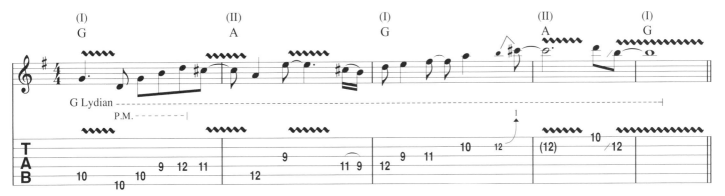

Mixolydian

Formula:	1–2–3–4–5–6–♭7
Construction:	W–W–H–W–W–H–W
Category:	major (sometimes called the dominant mode)
Differentiating scale degree:	♭7th
For chord types:	7; 9; 13; all 7sus4 types
Harmony:	I7–ii7–iii7♭5–IVmaj7–v7–vi7–♭VIImaj7
Common Progressions:	I–♭VII; I–♭VII–IV; I7–v; I7–IV; I–IV–♭VII–I; I7–I7sus4; I–vi–♭VII

Mixolydian outlines the basic structure of a dominant seventh chord (root, 3rd, 5th, ♭7th) and these extensions: 9th, 11th, and 13th.

Patterns for Mixolydian

(Roots are circled; notes in parentheses are the ♭7th degrees.)

Fig. 17

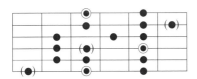  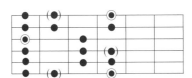

Mixolydian is the fifth mode of the major scale. It is sometimes referred to as the dominant mode because it corresponds to the V7 chord in major keys. But it also aligns with the ♭VII chord in minor key progressions.

The sound of Mixolydian is in the music all around us. The abundance of dominant seventh chords in the progressions of blues, funk, jazz, country, and rock make Mixolydian a popular choice among guitarists in those styles. Mixolydian is also a favorite of songwriters. Many a classic guitar riff has been culled from the Mixolydian mode—Roy Orbison's "Oh, Pretty Woman," The Beatles' "I Feel Fine," and "Birthday," and Jimi Hendrix's "Third Stone from the Sun," to name a few.

Mixolydian really comes alive in the dominant seventh jams of funk music. Fig. 18 offers an example of E Mixolydian in motion over an E9 vamp.

Fig. 18

E Mixolydian

Aeolian

Formula:	1–2–♭3–4–5–♭6–♭7
Construction:	W–H–W–W–H–W–W
Category:	minor
Differentiating scale degree:	♭6th
For chord types:	minor, m♭6, m7, m9, m11, m(add9)
Harmony:	i7–ii7♭5–♭IIImaj7–iv7–v7–♭VImaj7–♭VII7
Common Progressions:	i–♭VII–♭VI; i–iv; i–v; i–♭III–♭VII; i–♭VI

Aeolian outlines the basic structure of a minor seventh chord (root, ♭3rd, 5th, ♭7th) and these extensions: 9th, 11th, and ♭13th.

Patterns for Aeolian

(Roots are circled; notes in parentheses are the ♭6th degrees.)

Fig. 19

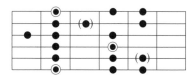
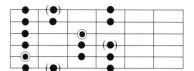
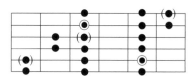

Aeolian is the modal name for the natural minor scale, and it is the mode that all other minor modes are compared to. It is the sixth mode of the major scale and corresponds to the vi chord in major keys. But its main role is to service the i chord in minor key progressions.

Common descriptions of the Aeolian mode include "romantic," "heavy," and "melodramatic"—small wonder it is such a favorite among hard-rock guitarists. Fig. 20 makes good use of the ♭6th degree of D Aeolian in a D minor rock ballad example.

Fig. 20

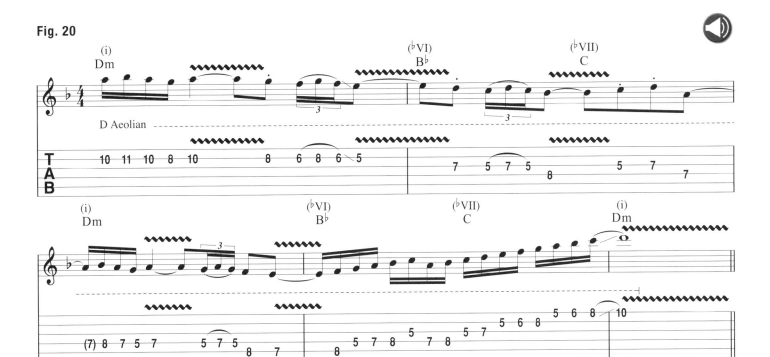

Locrian

Formula:	1–♭2–♭3–4–♭5–♭6–♭7
Construction:	H–W–W–H–W–W–W
Category:	minor (sometimes called the half-diminished mode)
Differentiating scale degree:	♭5th
For chord types:	diminished; m7♭5
Harmony:	i7♭5–♭IImaj7–♭iii7–iv7–♭Vmaj7–♭VI7–♭vii7
Common Progressions:	I°–♭II; i7♭5–iv7; i7♭5–♭vii7

Locrian outlines the basic structure of a minor seventh flat five chord (root, ♭3rd, ♭5th, ♭7th) and these extensions: ♭9th, 11th, and ♭13th.

Patterns for Locrian

(Roots are circled; notes in parentheses are the ♭5th degrees.)

Fig. 21

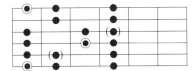 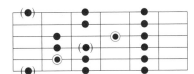 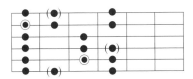

Locrian is the seventh mode of the major scale. It corresponds to the vii° chord in major keys, but it is most often relegated to the ii7♭5 chords in minor key progressions. When played out of context, it's a very strange sounding scale indeed. But when mated with a minor seven flat five chord, it nails all of the chord tones and provides some choice alterations (♭9th and ♭13th). Fig. 22 dispatches the B Locrian mode over the ii chord (Bm7♭5) in the key of A minor.

Fig. 22

 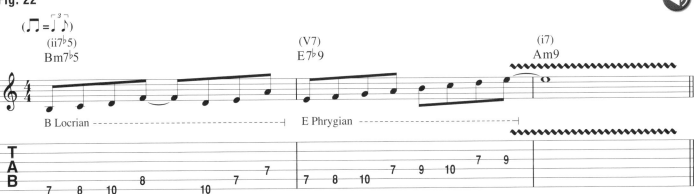

Quiz #11

(Answers are in the back of the book.)

1) What is the parent scale of G Dorian? _____

2) What is the parent scale of A Mixolydian? _____

3) What is the parent scale of C Lydian? _____

4) True or False: Dorian is a minor mode. _____

5) True or False: Lydian is a major mode. _____

6) Which mode is sometimes called the dominant mode? _____

7) What two modes have ♭2nd scale degrees? _____ _____

8) Which mode has a ♯4th scale degree? _____

9) What is the differentiating scale degree of Dorian? _____

10) What is the modal name for the major scale? _____

11) True or False: Lydian is very close in structure to the major scale. _____

12) True or False: Locrian is associated with the ii chord in minor keys. _____

Ear Training Drill #6

In each example you will hear one of the seven modes played in two octaves. Circle the correct answer. All examples start on the root. (Answers are in the back of the book.)

1) Ionian or Mixolydian?

2) Dorian or Phrygian?

3) Aeolian or Locrian?

4) Lydian or Ionian?

5) Mixolydian or Dorian?

6) Mixolydian or Ionian?

7) Phrygian or Locrian?

8) Ionian or Dorian?

9) Dorian or Aeolian?

10) Lydian or Mixolydian?

CHAPTER 12: OTHER SCALES AND MODES; CHORD/SCALE RELATIONSHIPS; ARPEGGIOS

OTHER SCALES AND MODES

Harmonic Minor

Formula:	1–2–♭3–4–5–♭6–7
Construction:	W–H–W–W–H–W+H–H
For Chord Types:	minor; m(maj7)
Harmony:	i(maj7)–ii7♭5–♭IIImaj7♯5–iv7–V7–♭VImaj7–vii°7

Fig. 1

A harmonic minor

Harmonic minor patterns

Harmonic minor is similar to the natural minor scale except that it has a raised 7th (major 7th) degree. This sharping of the 7th degree produces an unusual minor 3rd "gap" between the ♭6th and 7th scale degrees. The result is an "exotic" and assertive-sounding minor scale with an inherently strong sense of anticipation for resolution (return to the tonic).

In jazz, harmonic minor is a popular scale choice for soloing over m(maj7) chords. Harmonic minor is also a favorite among classical-influenced hard rock guitarists, who often use it as an alternative to Aeolian (natural minor).

Phrygian Dominant

(Fifth mode of harmonic minor)

Formula:	1–♭2–3–4–5–♭6–♭7
Construction:	H–W+H–H–W–H–W–W
For Chord Types:	Dom7 (functioning)

Fig. 2

A Phrygian Dominant

Phrygian Dominant patterns

Phrygian dominant is the fifth mode of the harmonic minor scale. It is very similar to the Phrygian mode (third mode) of the major scale. The only exception is that it has a major 3rd degree instead of a minor 3rd. Phrygian dominant is most often used over *functioning V chords* (chords which resolve to their respective I or i chord) in minor key progressions. Jazz, blues, and rock guitarists alike take advantage of the mode's chord-altering capabilities. For example, when the A Phrygian dominant scale (A–B♭–C♯–D–E–F–G) is super-imposed over an A7 chord, it outlines the root (A), 3rd (C♯), 5th (E), and ♭7th (G) of the chord, plus the alterations of a ♭9th (B♭), and a ♯5th or ♭13th (F). The D note serves as a "passing" 4th or 11th.

Melodic Minor (Jazz Melodic Minor)

Formula:	1–2–♭3–4–5–6–7
Construction:	W–H–W–W–W–W–H
For Chord Types:	minor; m(maj7)
Harmony:	i(maj7)–ii7–♭IIImaj7#5–IV7–V7–vi7♭5–vii7♭5

Fig. 3

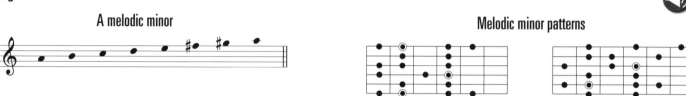

A melodic minor

Melodic minor patterns

The *melodic minor scale*—also referred to as the jazz melodic minor scale—can be likened to a major scale with a ♭3rd degree, but in terms of application it's more akin to the Dorian mode with a raised 7th (major 7th) degree. Like harmonic minor, melodic minor is used over m(maj7) chords, but it is also used by jazz and progressive blues players over minor seventh chords, as an alternative to Dorian. It is also a popular source for modes, as exhibited in the next four examples.

Lydian Dominant

(Fourth mode of melodic minor)

Formula:	1–2–3–#4–5–6–♭7
Construction:	W–W–W–H–W–H–W
For Chord Types:	Dom7#11

Fig. 4

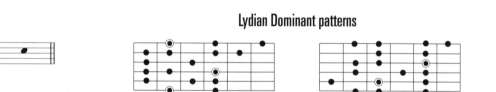

C Lydian Dominant

Lydian Dominant patterns

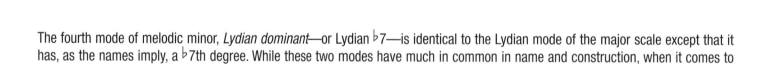

The fourth mode of melodic minor, *Lydian dominant*—or Lydian ♭7—is identical to the Lydian mode of the major scale except that it has, as the names imply, a ♭7th degree. While these two modes have much in common in name and construction, when it comes to application, Lydian dominant is more closely associated with Mixolydian.

Like Mixolydian, Lydian dominant can be used over dom7 chords, but it is an especially good match for dom7#11 chords. Since these chords are usually few and far between, many guitarists use Lydian dominant (as an alternative for Mixolydian) over dom7 and dom9 chords, employing the #4 as an altering device, much as they would the flat 5th of the blues scale.

Locrian #2

(Sixth mode of melodic minor)

Formula: 1–2–♭3–4–♭5–♭6–♭7

Construction: W–H–W–H–W–W–W

For Chord Types: m7♭5

Fig. 5

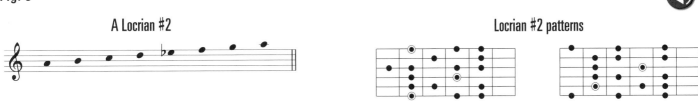

A Locrian #2   Locrian #2 patterns

Locrian #2, the sixth mode of melodic minor, is constructed just as its name suggests—like the Locrian mode (seventh mode of the major scale), but with a raised 2nd degree. Like the Locrian mode, its chief application is over m7♭5 chords.

Altered Scale (Super Locrian)

(Seventh mode of melodic minor)

Formula: 1–♭2–♭3–3–♭5–♭6–♭7

Construction: H–W–H–W–W–W–W

For Chord Types: Altered Dom7 (functioning)

Fig. 6

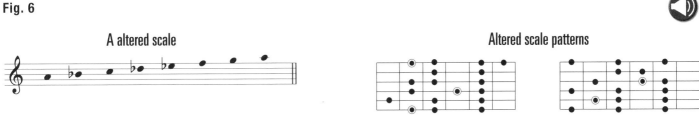

A altered scale   Altered scale patterns

The *altered scale*—or *Super Locrian*—is the seventh mode of the melodic minor scale. The altered scale is similar in construction to the Locrian mode, but whereas the latter contains a perfect 4th, the altered scale has a diminished 4th, which is enharmonic to a major 3rd degree. This results in the presence of both a minor 3rd and a major 3rd, but many players view the formula as 1–♭9–#9–3–♭5–#5–♭7. As you can see, all possible alterations are present: ♭9, #9, ♭5, and #5. Combined with its major 3rd and ♭7th degrees, this makes the altered scale an ideal choice for soloing over the functioning altered dominant chords in minor key chord progressions.

Lydian Augmented

(Third mode of melodic minor)

Formula:	1–2–3–#4–#5–6–7
Construction:	W–W–W–W–H–W–H
For Chord Types:	maj7#5

Fig. 7

C Lydian augmented

Lydian augmented patterns

Lydian augmented is the third mode of the melodic minor scale. As the name implies, it is constructed like Lydian, but with a raised 5th. It aligns perfectly with the major seventh sharp five chord, which often finds its way into the adventurous progressions of jazz-rock fusion.

Diminished (Whole-Half)

Formula:	1–2–♭3–4–♭5–♭6–♭♭7–7
Construction:	W–H–W–H–W–H–W–H
For Chord Types:	°7

Fig. 8

A diminished (whole/half)

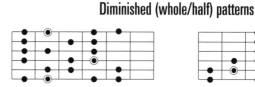

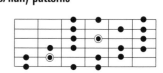

Diminished (whole/half) patterns

The *diminished (whole/half)* scale is a symmetrical (repetitive pattern of intervals) scale constructed with a series of alternating whole and half steps. This pattern results in a scale with eight tones. (Note: Like the °7 arpeggio, a diminished scale pattern repeats after every three frets on the fingerboard.) The diminished scale can be used over any °7 chord, regardless if the chord is the vii°7 of the key or if it's functioning as a passing chord. (Note: When writing the diminished scale on the staff, one letter name needs to be duplicated.)

Dominant Diminished (Half-Whole)

Formula:	1–♭2–♭3–3–#4–5–6–♭7
Construction:	H–W–H–W–H–W–H–W
For Chord Types:	Dom13 (functioning)

Fig. 9

A diminished (half/whole)

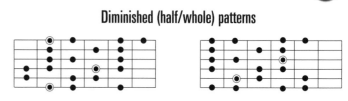

Diminished (half/whole) patterns

The *dominant diminished (half/whole) scale* can be viewed as being the second, and only, mode of the diminished whole/half scale. That is, if you start on either the 2nd, 4th, 6th, or 7th scale degree of the diminished whole/half scale and play up an octave, you'll be creating a half/whole formula. When superimposed over a dom7 chord, the dominant diminished scale outlines the basic quality of the chord (root, 3rd, 5th, and ♭7th) plus the extension of a 13th, and the alterations of a ♭9th, ♯9th, and ♭5th. This makes the scale perfect for the dom13♭9 chords so prevalent in the major key progressions in jazz, but it can actually be used over any functioning V chord that doesn't include a ♯5th alteration.

Whole Tone

Formula:	1–2–3–♯4–♯5–♭7
Construction:	W–W–W–W–W–W
For Chord Types:	augmented

Fig. 10

C whole tone scale

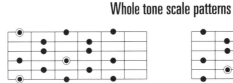

Whole tone scale patterns

Yet another popular symmetrical scale is the whole tone scale. It is comprised solely of whole step intervals and contains only six notes. It can be quite useful when applied over augmented chords—particularly those of the functioning V variety. (When writing the whole tone scale on the staff, one letter name is omitted.)

Chromatic Scale

Formula:	1–♭2–2–♭3–3–4–♭5–5–♭6–6–♭7–7
Construction:	H–H–H–H–H–H–H–H–H–H–H

Fig. 11

C chromatic scale

Demonstrated in two octaves on the audio track.

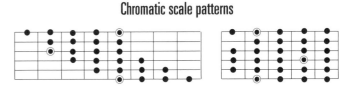

Chromatic scale patterns

The *chromatic scale* is a twelve-tone scale that includes every half step interval within an octave. It is usually used in smaller sections, within the context of diatonic scales, for the purpose of creating altered scale tones (tones outside the scale). This is common practice among jazz (particularly in bebop) and hot country guitarists. Chromatic sequences are also common fixtures in classic hard rock.

CHORD/SCALE RELATIONSHIPS

Chord/scale relationship soloing involves treating the chords in a progression as separate entities, and using a different scale for each. Chord/scale relationship information is interspersed throughout this book, but this section gathers the data, and puts it into one convenient reference chart. The chart is separated into three main sections: Major, Minor, and Dominant. Bear in mind, the scales are merely suggestions—there are always other possibilities. The choice is ultimately up to the player.

Major Category

Group 1

Chord type: Major-triad chord types, with or without extensions
Chord name: C, C6, Cadd9, C6/9, Cadd4
Suggested scales: C major pentatonic, or C major pentatonic add4 (C major scale, no 7th)

Group 2

Chord type: Major seventh chords
Chord name: Cmaj7, Cmaj9, Cmaj13
Suggested scale: C major scale

Group 3

Chord type: Altered major chords
Chord name: C6/9#11, Cmaj7#11, Cmaj9#11, Cmaj13#11
Suggested scale: C Lydian

Chord name: Cmaj7#5, Cmaj9#5, Cmaj13#5
Suggested scale: C Lydian augmented

Minor Category

Group 1

Chord type: Minor chord types with no 6ths and without alterations
Chord name: Cm, Cm(add9), Cm7, Cm9, Cm11
Suggested scales: C minor pentatonic, C minor pentatonic add9 (C minor hexatonic), C natural minor scale (Aeolian mode)

Group 2

Chord type: Minor sixth chord types
Chord name: Cm6, Cm6/9, Cm13
Suggested scale: C Dorian

Group 3

Chord type: Minor chords with alterations
Chord name: Cm7♭5
Suggested scales: C Locrian, C Locrian #2

Chord name: Cm(maj7), Cm(maj9)
Suggested scales: C harmonic minor, C melodic minor

Chord name: C°7
Suggested scale: C diminished (whole/half)

Dominant Category

Group 1

Chord type: Non-altered dominant chords
Chord name: C7, C9, C13, C7sus4, C9sus4, C13sus4, C11
Suggested scales: C Mixolydian

Group 2

Chord type: Dominant chords with altered 5ths
Chord name: C+7, C7♭5, C+9, C9♭5
Suggested scale: C whole tone

Chord type: Dominant chords with ♯11ths
Chord name: C7♯11, C9♯11
Suggested scale: C Lydian dominant

Group 3

Chord type: Dominant chords with altered 9ths
Chord name: C7♭9, C+7♭9
Suggested scales: C Phrygian dominant, C altered scale, C Phrygian

Chord name: C7♯9
Suggested scales: C minor pentatonic, C blues scale

Chord name: C13♭9, C13♯9
Suggested scale: C dominant diminished (half/whole)

ARPEGGIOS

An arpeggio is a chord whose notes are played in succession (one at a time), rather than simultaneously. From a rhythm standpoint, basic arpeggios are really quite simple: choose any chord voicing and play it one string at a time, in any combination (Fig. 12).

Fig. 12

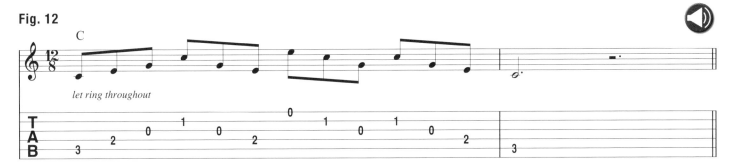

More often though, guitarists use arpeggios for soloing purposes. Arpeggios are among the most melodic devices available to the lead guitarist. Not only are they a great source for constructing beautifully flowing phrases, they are also invaluable devices for "nailing the changes" of virtually any style of chord progression.

Triad Arpeggio Patterns

Minor triad arpeggios are very popular among blues and rock guitarists. This is probably because they coincide so well with minor pentatonic scales. Strip away the 4th and the ♭7th of any minor pentatonic scale pattern, and you'll have a minor triad arpeggio pattern. Fig. 13 shows two patterns of an A minor triad arpeggio. See the similarities?

Fig. 13

A minor triad arpeggios

Major triad arpeggios go hand in hand with major pentatonic scales. You'll hear them in country and country rock, as well as blues and rock. Fig. 14 shows two patterns of C major triad arpeggios.

Fig. 14

C major triad arpeggios

Seventh Arpeggio Patterns

Seventh arpeggios are more colorful than triad arpeggios. Popular among jazz and classically-influenced rock guitarists, they can be used to nail the chord tones of changes, as well as to suggest the entire tonality of scales and modes.

Just as there are four basic seventh chords, there are four basic seventh arpeggios: major seventh, minor seventh, dominant seventh, and minor seven flat five. Figs. 15–18 show two patterns of each arpeggio, all in C. Each is designed to align with its corresponding chord (Cmaj7 arpeggio over a Cmaj7 chord, Cm7♭5 arpeggio over a Cm7♭5 chord, etc.)

Figs. 15–18

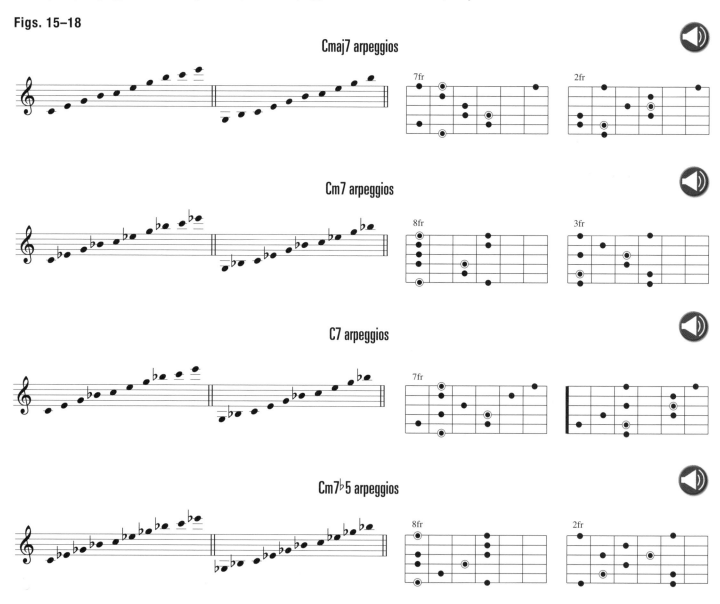

Cmaj7 arpeggios

Cm7 arpeggios

C7 arpeggios

Cm7♭5 arpeggios

It's good to practice arpeggio patterns in their entirety, but, just like scales, the notes should be used selectively for a melodic outcome. It's also common practice to add extensions and alterations to these basic arpeggios. Some guitarists link the notes of arpeggios with short, chromatic passages.

Quiz #12

This is a true-or-false quiz. (Answers are in the back of the book.)

1) Harmonic minor is a minor scale with a raised seventh degree. _____

2) Phrygian dominant is a mode of the major scale. _____

3) Melodic minor is like the Dorian mode, but with a raised seventh degree. _____

4) Lydian dominant is a mode of melodic minor. _____

5) Locrian #2 is a good scale choice for major seventh chords. _____

6) The altered scale contains all possible alterations. _____

7) The diminished scale is a series of whole step intervals. _____

8) The whole tone scale contains six notes. _____

9) The chromatic scale is a diatonic scale. _____

10) When you play the notes of a chord one at a time it's called an arpeggio. _____

11) A Cmaj7 arpeggio is the perfect compliment for a Cmaj7 chord. _____

Ear Training Drill #7

In Section A you will hear a scale played in two octaves. All examples start on the root of the scale. Circle the correct answer. (Answers are in the back of the book.)

Section A

1) Harmonic minor or the major scale?

2) Melodic minor or Dorian?

3) The whole tone scale or diminished (whole/half)?

4) The dominant diminished (half/whole) scale or Phrygian?

5) The altered scale or Lydian dominant?

6) Locrian #2 or Mixolydian?

7) Lydian augmented or the chromatic scale?

8) Phrygian dominant or the altered scale?

9) Altered scale or Aeolian?

In Section B you will hear an arpeggio played in two octaves. All arpeggios start on the root. Circle the correct answer.

Section B

10) Major or minor triad arpeggio?

11) Major triad or major seventh arpeggio?

12) Major seventh or minor seventh arpeggio?

13) Minor seven flat five or dominant seventh arpeggio?

14) Dominant seventh or major seventh arpeggio?

15) Minor or major triad arpeggio?

CHAPTER 13: CHORD SUBSTITUTIONS AND REHARMONIZATION

Chord substitution is a musical way to "dress up" chords and chord progressions. These substitution methods range from simple to extremely complex.

CHORD EMBELLISHMENT

Chord embellishment (also known as *direct substitution*) is the most basic type of substitution. This is where you embellish a chord with added notes, such as extensions. Cadd9 would be a direct substitute for a C chord; C9 could stand in for a C7 chord; and Cm9 could substitute for a Cm7 chord (Fig. 1). The main thing to remember with direct substitution is not to change the basic quality of the chord.

Fig. 1

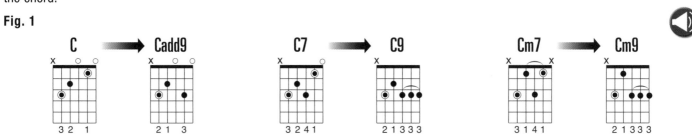

DIATONIC CHORD SUBSTITUTION AND REHARMONIZATION

Diatonic chord *substitution* is when a different chord from the same harmonized scale is substituted for another. The rules for diatonic substitution lie in a system of three groups called *chord families*. These three families are based on the I, IV, and V chords of the major scale. The family of the I chord is called the tonic family. Its basic role in a progression is to temporarily or permanently resolve the key. The family of the IV chord is called the *subdominant* family. The subdominant family creates the feeling of moving away from the I chord. The family of the V chord is the *dominant* family. The dominant family has the effect of moving toward (or resolving to) the I chord. (The chief reason for this is the dominant family chords contain the *leading tone*, or the 7th degree of the scale, which has a strong pull toward the tonic.)

The family relationship depends on how much the other chords resemble either the I, IV, or V in structure—in other words, how many notes they have in common. If you line up the diatonic triads from C major on the staff (Fig. 2) the similarities are evident.

Fig. 2

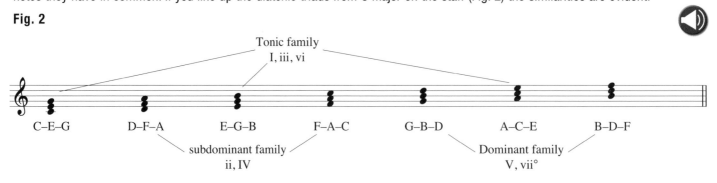

The major key diatonic chord families are as follows:

Family	Triads	Seventh Chords
Tonic	I, iii, and vi	Imaj7, iii7, vi7
Subdominant	IV and ii	IVmaj7 and ii7
Dominant	V and vii°	V7 and vii7♭5

Let's use this information to reharmonize the following C major progression (Figs. 3A–3B). (*Reharmonization* is the process of exchanging related chords to create a different sounding progression.)

Figs. 3A–3B

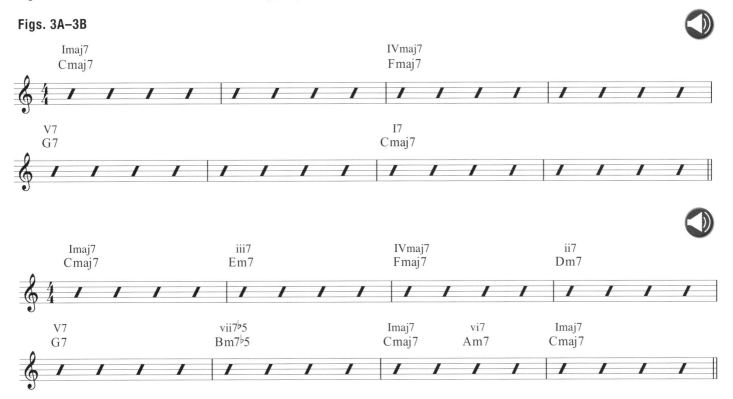

The minor scale also contains chord families, but they are slightly different:

Family	Triads	Seventh Chords
Tonic	i and ♭III	i7 and ♭IIImaj7
Subdominant	iv, ii°, and ♭VI	iv7, ii7♭5, and ♭VImaj7
Dominant	v and ♭VII	v7 and ♭VIImaj7

Let's use this information to reharmonize the following D minor progression (Fig. 4A–4B).

Figs. 4A–4B

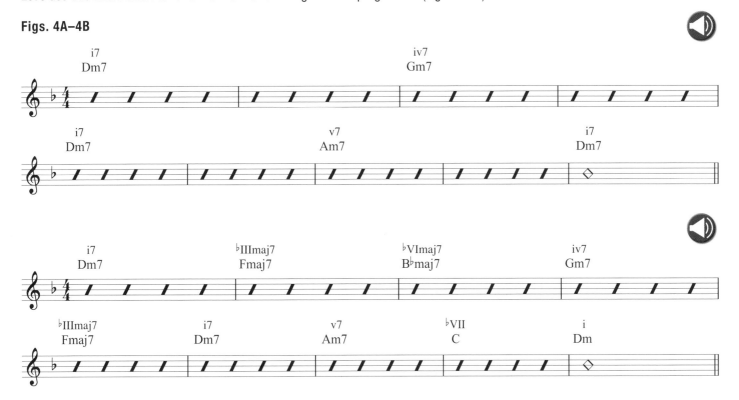

Triad and Seventh Arpeggio Substitution

Diatonic substitution methods work for triads and seventh arpeggios too. Simply apply the chord family concepts to arpeggios. For example, in the key of C major, an Em7 arpeggio could be substituted over a Cmaj7; a Bm7♭5 arpeggio could be substituted over a G7 chord; or an Fmaj7 arpeggio could be substituted over the Dm7 (ii7) chord. This is also referred to as *melodic substitution*.

Another form of substitution is when two or more triads or seventh arpeggios are superimposed over a single chord or a key center. For example, Cmaj7, Em7, and Am7 arpeggios might all be played in succession over a Cmaj7 (Fig. 5A). Some players go so far as to superimpose all of the triads or arpeggios in a key over a single chord. Fig. 5B superimposes all of the triads from the A minor scale over an Am7 chord.

Fig. 5A

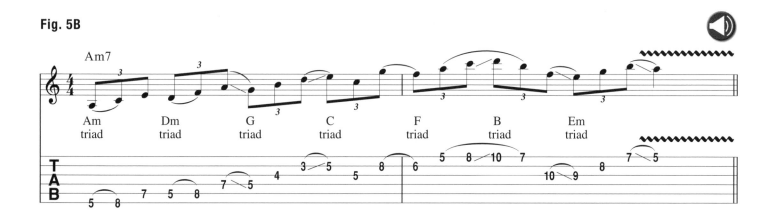

Fig. 5B

Flat-Five Substitution

Flat-five substitution—or *tritone substitution*—occurs when a functioning dominant seventh chord is replaced with one whose root is a flat 5th—or tritone—away. Fig. 6 illustrates this process on the staff in a ii–V–I progression in the key of C.

Fig. 6

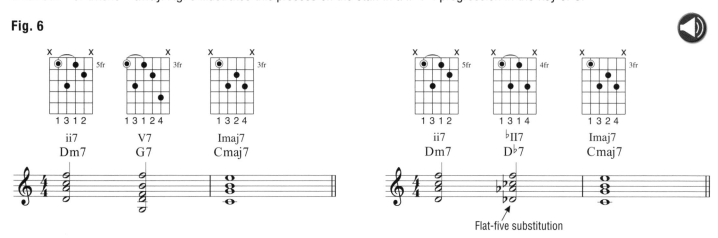

Notice that the D♭7 chord retains the "heart" of the G7 chord (B and F; 3rd and ♭7th) while creating a descending bassline in the progression (D–D♭–C). Tritone substitution can also be applied to major triads and dominant seventh arpeggios. For example, in the above progression, a D♭ triad or a D♭7 arpeggio could substitute for the G7.

Secondary Dominant Substitution

A *secondary dominant* is related to direct substitution, where a chord containing the same root and basic quality is substituted for another (C6/9 is a direct substitute for C6). With secondary dominant chords however, the basic chord quality is changed from either major or minor to dominant. For example, in a C major progression, a C7 would be a secondary dominant substitute for the I chord; a D7 chord would be a secondary dominant substitute for the ii chord; and so on.

Secondary dominant chords are common in styles such as R&B, gospel, jazz, and turn-of-the-century "pizza-parlor" songs. Secondary dominant chords often resolve up a 4th, or down a 5th, to the next chord in the progression. When this occurs, the chord is called a functioning secondary dominant.

Fig. 7 provides examples of functioning and non-functioning secondary dominant chords.

Fig. 7

Diminished Seventh Chord Substitution

Diminished seventh chord substitution has its roots in the harmony of the harmonic minor scale (see Chapter 12). For example, the vii° chord in A harmonic minor is G#°7; and the V chord is E7. Using the "chord family" principle, these two chords are both in the dominant family and, consequently, can substitute for one another. Incidentally, they also contain the *leading tone* (G#) of the scale (Fig. 8).

Fig. 8

Because of their similar structure, diminished seventh chords often stand in for dominant seventh chords. For instance, in the key of C, a B°7 could be substituted for a G7 chord. Since the B°7 chord is based on the leading tone of the key, the result still has a V–I resolution effect (Fig. 9).

Fig. 9

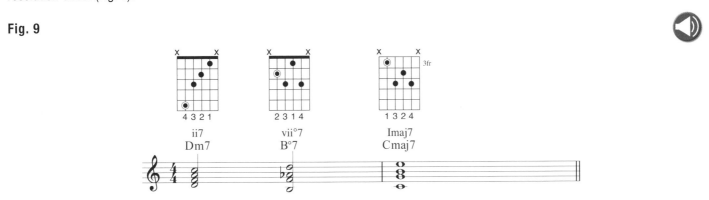

Diminished seventh chords are also used as substitutes for functioning secondary dominant chords, as illustrated in (Fig. 10). Notice that the root of each diminished chord is the "leading tone" of the next chord. (Note: The vii°7/ii analysis means the C#°7 is functioning as the vii°7 of the ii chord in the progression. The D#°7 is the vii°7 of the iii chord.)

Fig. 10

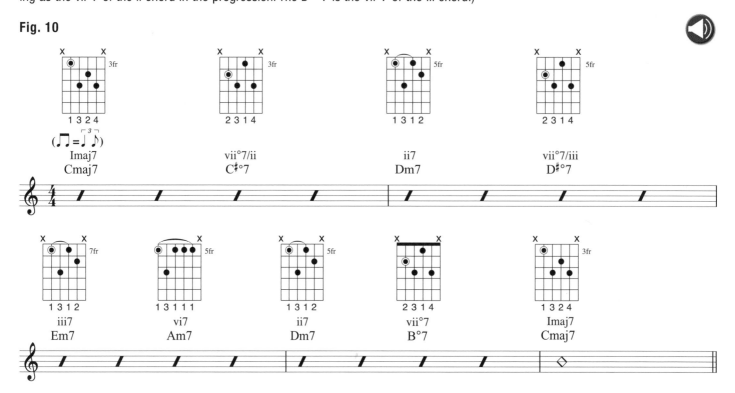

By the way, these diminished substitution concepts can be applied to diminished seventh arpeggios as well.

Quiz #13

1)   What are the triad chords in the tonic family of the major scale? ___ ___ ___

2)   What are the triad chords in the tonic family of the minor scale? ___ ___

3)   What are the seventh chords in the subdominant family of the major scale? ___ ___

4)   What are the seventh chords in the dominant family of the major scale? ___ ___

5)   True or false—G7 contains the leading tone of C major. _____

6)   True or false—A7 is a secondary dominant chord in the key of C. _____

7)   True or false—In the key of C, Bm7♭5 is a diatonic substitution for G7. _____

8)   True or false—In the key of C, E♭m7 is a diatonic substitute for Cmaj7. _____

9)   True or false—In a C major progression, D#°7 is the vii°7 of the iii chord (Em7). _____

10) True or false—A *functioning* secondary dominant chord resolves to its respective I or i chord in a progression. _____

11) True or false—In the key of F, G♭7 could be used as a flat-five substitute for the V chord (C7). _____

INDEX OF MUSICAL TERMS

ANSWER KEYS FOR QUIZZES AND EAR TRAINING DRILLS

CHAPTER 2
Answers for Quiz #1

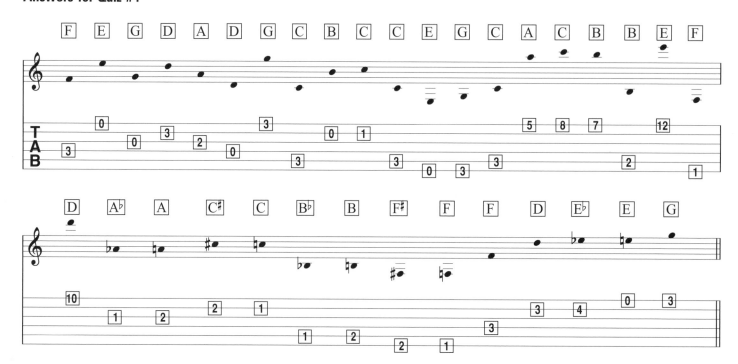

Answers for Quiz #2

CHAPTER 3
Answers for Quiz #3

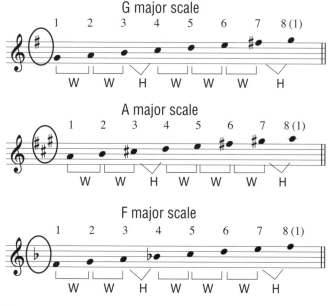

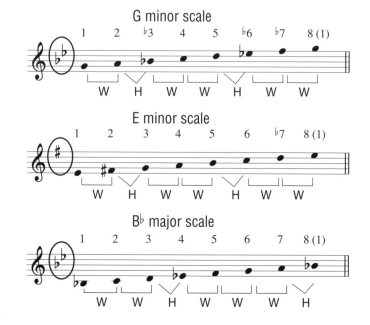

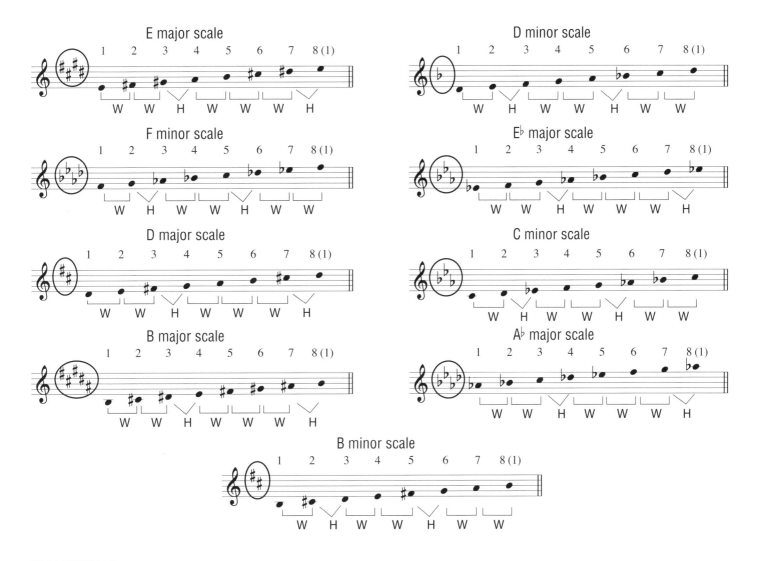

CHAPTER 4

Answers for Quiz #4

P 4th   P 4th   maj 3rd   mi 3rd   P 5th   P octave   mi 7th   mi 2nd   maj 6th   mi 6th

mi 7th   aug 4th   maj 3rd   maj 3rd   dim 5th   P 5th   maj 3rd   maj 10th   P 11th   maj 13th

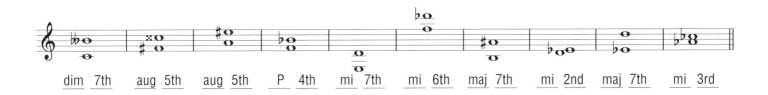

dim 7th   aug 5th   aug 5th   P 4th   mi 7th   mi 6th   maj 7th   mi 2nd   maj 7th   mi 3rd

Answers for Ear Training Drill #1 (three sections)

Fig. 11

#1 minor 2nd   #2 major 3rd   #3 major 2nd   #4 minor 3rd

#5 minor 3rd   #6 minor 2nd   #7 minor 2nd   #8 major 3rd

Fig. 12

#1 perfect 4th   #2 perfect 5th   #3 diminished 5th   #4 octave

#5 perfect 4th   #6 perfect 5th   #7 octave   #8 diminished 5th

Fig. 13

#1 major 6th   #2 major 7th   #3 minor 7th   #4 major 6th

#5 minor 6th   #6 major 7th   #7 minor 7th   #8 minor 6th

CHAPTER 5

Answers for Quiz #5

1. Emaj   2. E+   3. Fm   4. F°   5. Gm   6. Dm   7. D+   8. Cm   9. A♭maj   10. F♯m   11. B+   12. E♭°

Answers for Quiz #6

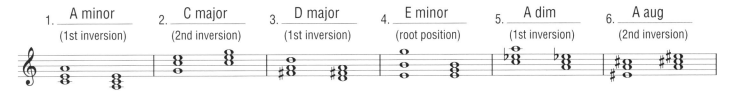

1. A minor (1st inversion)   2. C major (2nd inversion)   3. D major (1st inversion)   4. E minor (root position)   5. A dim (1st inversion)   6. A aug (2nd inversion)

7. C major (root position)   8. G minor (1st inversion)   9. F major (2nd inversion)   10. G dim (1st inversion)   11. E major (1st inversion)   12. B minor (1st inversion)

Answers for Ear Training Drill #2 (three sections)

Fig. 14A

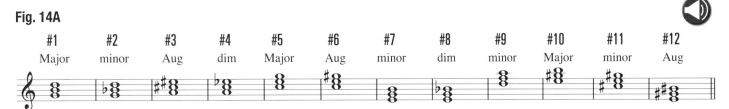

#1	#2	#3	#4	#5	#6	#7	#8	#9	#10	#11	#12
Major	minor	Aug	dim	Major	Aug	minor	dim	minor	Major	minor	Aug

Fig. 14B

#1	#2	#3	#4	#5	#6	#7	#8	#9	#10	#11	#12
Major	Major	minor	minor	Major	minor	Major	minor	minor	Major	minor	Major

Fig. 14C

#1	#2	#3	#4	#5	#6	#7	#8	#9	#10	#11	#12
Major	minor	Major	minor	minor	Major	Major	minor	Major	Major	minor	minor

CHAPTER 6

Answers for Quiz #7

1) Dominant seventh chord

2) Minor seventh chord

3) Minor seventh flat five chord

4) Major seventh chord

5) B7

6) They are all minor seventh in quality

7) G°

8) G, C, and D

9) Amaj7, Dmaj7, and E7

10) F–Dm–B♭–C

11) Dm7

12) C♯m7

CHAPTER 7
Answers for Quiz #8

1) Major triad
2) Diminished triad
3) Minor seventh
4) Dominant
5) C

6) No
7) A–C–E♭–G♭
8) C9sus4
9) G/B
10) False

CHAPTER 8
Answers for Quiz #9

1) Am and Bm
2) B
3) B♭maj7
4) Bm7
5) Gm7–Cm7–Dm7
6) Gmaj7–Cmaj7–D7

7) G#°
8) G
9) E minor
10) D major
11) I
12) i

Answers for Ear Training Drill #3

A. 1) major
   2) minor
   3) minor
   4) major
   5) major
   6) minor
   7) major
B. 8) major
   9) minor
   10) minor
   11) major

   12) minor
   13) major
   14) major
C. 15) major
   16) minor
   17) minor
   18) major
   19) minor
   20) major
   21) major

CHAPTER 9
Answers for Ear Training Drill #4

Major or Minor Progressions:

1) Major
2) Minor
3) Minor
4) Major

5) Major
6) Major
7) Minor
8) Minor

Modal Interchange:

1) Yes
2) No
3) Yes

4) Yes
5) No

CHAPTER 10
Answers for Quiz #10

1) The IV chord
2) In measure 2
3) In measures 11 and 12
4) Five
5) None
6) Six

7) The IV chord
8) 1–2–3–5–6
9) Dominant seventh
10) C major
11) A major

Answers for Ear Training Drill #5

1) minor pentatonic
2) major pentatonic
3) blues scale
4) major pentatonic
5) blues scale
6) minor pentatonic

7) minor pentatonic
8) blues scale
9) major pentatonic
10) blues scale
11) major pentatonic
12) minor pentatonic

CHAPTER 11
Answers for Quiz #11

1) F major
2) D major
3) G major
4) True
5) True
6) Mixolydian

7) Phrygian and Locrian
8) Lydian
9) 6th
10) Ionian
11) True
12) True

Answers for Ear Training Drill #6

1) Ionian
2) Dorian
3) Aeolian
4) Lydian
5) Mixolydian

6) Mixolydian
7) Locrian
8) Dorian
9) Aeolian
10) Lydian

CHAPTER 12
Answers for Quiz #12

1) True
2) False
3) True
4) True
5) False
6) True

7) False
8) True
9) False
10) True
11) True

Answers for Ear Training Drill #7

A. 1) Harmonic minor
   2) Melodic minor
   3) Diminished (whole/half)
   4) Dominant diminished (half/whole)
   5) Lydian dominant
   6) Locrian #2
   7) Chromatic scale
   8) Phrygian dominant
   9) Altered scale

B. 10) Major
   11) Major 7th
   12) Minor 7th
   13) Minor 7♭5
   14) Dominant 7th
   15) Minor

CHAPTER 13

Answers for Quiz #13

1) I, iii, and vi
2) i and ♭III
3) IVmaj7 and ii7
4) V7 and vii7♭5
5) True
6) True

7) True
8) False
9) True
10) True
11) True

Guitar Notation Legend

Guitar Music can be notated three different ways: on a *musical staff*, in *tablature*, and in *rhythm slashes*.

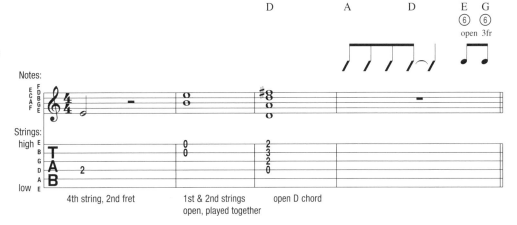

RHYTHM SLASHES are written above the staff. Strum chords in the rhythm indicated. Use the chord diagrams found at the top of the first page of the transcription for the appropriate chord voicings. Round noteheads indicate single notes.

THE MUSICAL STAFF shows pitches and rhythms and is divided by bar lines into measures. Pitches are named after the first seven letters of the alphabet.

TABLATURE graphically represents the guitar fingerboard. Each horizontal line represents a a string, and each number represents a fret.

4th string, 2nd fret

1st & 2nd strings open, played together

open D chord

Definitions for Special Guitar Notation

HALF-STEP BEND: Strike the note and bend up 1/2 step.

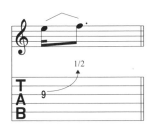

WHOLE-STEP BEND: Strike the note and bend up one step.

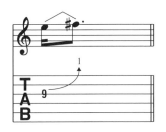

GRACE NOTE BEND: Strike the note and immediately bend up as indicated.

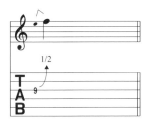

SLIGHT (MICROTONE) BEND: Strike the note and bend up 1/4 step.

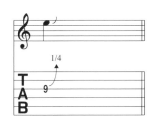

BEND AND RELEASE: Strike the note and bend up as indicated, then release back to the original note. Only the first note is struck.

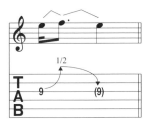

PRE-BEND: Bend the note as indicated, then strike it.

PRE-BEND AND RELEASE: Bend the note as indicated. Strike it and release the bend back to the original note.

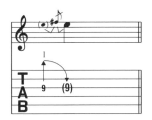

UNISON BEND: Strike the two notes simultaneously and bend the lower note up to the pitch of the higher.

VIBRATO: The string is vibrated by rapidly bending and releasing the note with the fretting hand.

WIDE VIBRATO: The pitch is varied to a greater degree by vibrating with the fretting hand.

HAMMER-ON: Strike the first (lower) note with one finger, then sound the higher note (on the same string) with another finger by fretting it without picking.

PULL-OFF: Place both fingers on the notes to be sounded. Strike the first note and without picking, pull the finger off to sound the second (lower) note.

LEGATO SLIDE: Strike the first note and then slide the same fret-hand finger up or down to the second note. The second note is not struck.

SHIFT SLIDE: Same as legato slide, except the second note is struck.

TRILL: Very rapidly alternate between the notes indicated by continuously hammering on and pulling off.

TAPPING: Hammer ("tap") the fret indicated with the pick-hand index or middle finger and pull off to the note fretted by the fret hand.

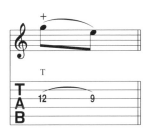

NATURAL HARMONIC: Strike the note while the fret-hand lightly touches the string directly over the fret indicated.

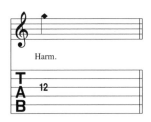

PINCH HARMONIC: The note is fretted normally and a harmonic is produced by adding the edge of the thumb or the tip of the index finger of the pick hand to the normal pick attack.

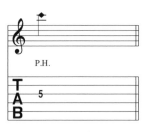

HARP HARMONIC: The note is fretted normally and a harmonic is produced by gently resting the pick hand's index finger directly above the indicated fret (in parentheses) while the pick hand's thumb or pick assists by plucking the appropriate string.

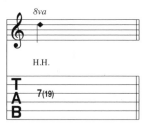

PICK SCRAPE: The edge of the pick is rubbed down (or up) the string, producing a scratchy sound.

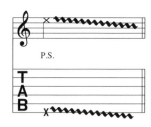

MUFFLED STRINGS: A percussive sound is produced by laying the fret hand across the string(s) without depressing, and striking them with the pick hand.

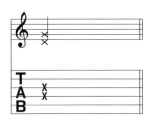

PALM MUTING: The note is partially muted by the pick hand lightly touching the string(s) just before the bridge.

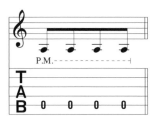

RAKE: Drag the pick across the strings indicated with a single motion.

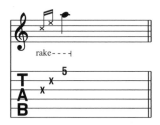

TREMOLO PICKING: The note is picked as rapidly and continuously as possible.

ARPEGGIATE: Play the notes of the chord indicated by quickly rolling them from bottom to top.

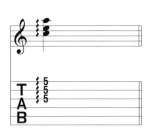

VIBRATO BAR DIVE AND RETURN: The pitch of the note or chord is dropped a specified number of steps (in rhythm) then returned to the original pitch.

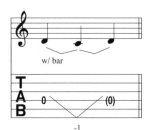

VIBRATO BAR SCOOP: Depress the bar just before striking the note, then quickly release the bar.

VIBRATO BAR DIP: Strike the note and then immediately drop a specified number of steps, then release back to the original pitch.

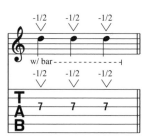

Additional Musical Definitions

 (accent) • Accentuate note (play it louder)

 (accent) • Accentuate note with great intensity

 (staccato) • Play the note short

⊓ • Downstroke

∨ • Upstroke

D.S. al Coda • Go back to the sign (𝄋), then play until the measure marked "**To Coda**," then skip to the section labelled "**Coda**."

D.C. al Fine • Go back to the beginning of the song and play until the measure marked "**Fine**" (end).

Rhy. Fig. • Label used to recall a recurring accompaniment pattern (usually chordal).

Riff • Label used to recall composed, melodic lines (usually single notes) which recur.

Fill • Label used to identify a brief melodic figure which is to be inserted into the arrangement.

Rhy. Fill • A chordal version of a Fill.

tacet • Instrument is silent (drops out).

 • Repeat measures between signs.

 • When a repeated section has different endings, play the first ending only the first time and the second ending only the second time.

NOTE: Tablature numbers in parentheses mean:
1. The note is being sustained over a system (note in standard notation is tied), or
2. The note is sustained, but a new articulation (such as a hammer-on, pull-off, slide or vibrato begins), or
3. The note is a barely audible "ghost" note (note in standard notation is also in parentheses).